RESHAPING
THE TEACHING MINISTRY

RESHAPING THE TEACHING MINISTRY

Toward Relevant Education in the Local Congregation

By Paul M. Lederach

 HERALD PRESS, SCOTTDALE, PENNSYLVANIA

The quotation on pages 33, 34 was taken from *How to Become a Bishop Without Being Religious* by Charles Merrill Smith. Copyright © 1965 by Charles Merrill Smith. Reprinted·by permission of Doubleday & Company, Inc.

RESHAPING THE TEACHING MINISTRY

Copyright © 1968 by Herald Press, Scottdale, Pa. 15683
Library of Congress Catalog Card Number: 68-22266
Printed in the United States

To
My Wife, Mary

Foreword

To think about and work in the field of Christian education is exciting in this latter third of the twentieth century.
One reason is, Christian education is in transition. The old
ways, we are beginning to see, are not equal to these times.
Here and there churchmen are taking a hard look at the
church's teaching ministry. The criticisms, experiments, and
the suggestions for new forms are tantalizing. It is in this
context of critique and experimentation that we will explore the teaching ministry of the church.

Since the early fifties, the Mennonite Church and the
General Conference Mennonite Church have been working
cooperatively in Christian education curriculum preparation.
Our experiences have been exciting, both as we have come
to know each other more deeply and as we have explored
together the ferment in Christian education.

After working jointly on Uniform Sunday School revision,
our major cooperative venture was the creation of a graded
Sunday school series. This task forced us to ask what Christian education is about within the Anabaptist tradition. In
the graded project, our first task was the development of
objectives. Here we settled upon twelve areas of outcomes.
These areas were spelled out across the life-span from
primaries to young people. The book containing objectives

7

is an interesting document. These objectives provided the background for developing the graded curriculum.

When planning the curriculum, I can remember the diligent work as the group tried to bring focus into the graded series through themes. The themes we selected do indeed reflect the essence of Anabaptist theology. Perhaps here, more than any one place, we sensed the leading of the Spirit as we agreed on Redemption, Church, and Discipleship. The longer we worked with the curriculum, the more convinced we became that these themes are at the heart of our tradition. In 1954, we outlined the curriculum. In 1956, writers began to work. And in 1959, the first of the materials appeared. By 1962 the entire series was released.

In the meantime the world refused to stand still. No sooner was the project completed than parts became obsolete. There are many reasons for this. Many denominations were in the midst of reappraisal. A major contribution to new conceptualizations of Christian education was the Cooperative Curriculum Projective, a joint venture of sixteen denominations. We, too, began looking at Christian education in a different way. Some of us received new light on the nature of the church. We saw a bit more clearly the mission of the church in the world and her ministry of reconciliation. We saw that the church functions on one hand as a gathered community and on the other hand as a scattered community when believers are dispersed and move in the world. Harold S. Bender, in *These Are My People*, referred to the "internal" and to the "external" ministries. These notions began to work at the very foundations of the current teaching ministry. Up to this time, the educational program was in the form of building blocks: one agency\built upon another, or side by side. Persons were invited to "come" to our structures. We saw that this motif needed to be changed; we came to see the congregation functioning as a body in the world. Instead of "come," "go" becomes the motif. This led us to see that the teaching ministry must undergird the congregation—prepare people or equip them for service and witness in the world as well as functioning when the congregation gathers.

These insights came almost like conversion. No longer was Christian education seen as an end in itself, a paradise for those who love to tinker with structures and make things bigger and better, or who love to carry a satchel full of gimmicks. These insights led to a painful meeting of the Mennonite Commission for Christian Education in 1962, when it took a look at the establishment. What it saw led to a more profound dissatisfaction. This led to a cooperative seminar at Bethel College, Newton, Kansas, in 1963. Here things began to fall together again as we developed a new objective for Christian education. Since 1963, we have been attempting to understand the implications of this objective. The objective is as follows:

Through Christian education the church seeks to help all persons to know God as revealed supremely in Jesus Christ and the Scriptures: to become aware of who they are, of what their situation is, and of their alienation to the end that they may repent of their sin, respond to God's redeeming love in faith, and become members of the body of Christ; to grow in Christ within the community of believers, to walk in the Spirit in every relationship, to fulfill the call to discipleship in the world, and to abide in the Christian hope.

This objective, which has been at the heart of our thinking since 1963, has been a Pandora's box. It has opened up many new insights as we have taken it seriously. In the summer of 1965, we tried to look at the meaning of the objective for the congregation's teaching program. For the first time we looked at Christian education holistically. Those trying to do Christian education talked with those working in areas such as peace, social and economic concerns, and missions with a focus on serving the local congregation and helping it overcome its fragmented teaching ministry. The group sensed that Christian education must be brought into focus, that it must undergird the congregation in its mission, and prepare each member for his task.

Now we are engaged cooperatively in thinking through a new curriculum for adults and for children four and five years of age. We are taking seriously new insights in Christian education growing out of the objective and of our understanding of the nature and purpose of the church. Now we are trying to consolidate new insights and sense of direction into a new program.

I was grateful for the request of the Canadian Mennonite Bible College, Winnipeg, Manitoba, to prepare and present a series of lectures in the field of Christian education. This provided the opportunity to bring into some order the ideas we have been dealing with and to make articulate some of the forces that have been pushing beneath the surface. These lectures resulted in this book. Throughout this book the learned apparatus is very irregular.

In most places, contentions are unsupported by famous names. Thus, this study is only half a serious study. Whether the contentions are accepted or rejected is not important. What is important is that persons think anew concerning some of the issues in Christian education. Though structures are questioned, the foundation which is laid, Jesus Christ, stands sure. He is the source, the resource, and the end of the teaching ministry. And the church, of which He is head, is composed of those who are "God's children now" (1 John 3:2) and yet are in the process of becoming, "with unveiled face, beholding the glory of the Lord, are being changed into his likeness from one degree of glory to another" (2 Corinthians 3:18).

Introduction

Any evaluation of the current scene in Christian education will be determined in large part by the perspective from which it is viewed. For some people the very fact of change is most alarming, for in their estimation this in itself means deterioration and ruin. In the field of Christian education they feel it means leaving the basic and staid foundations we once knew to be cast adrift on a windswept ocean with no course to follow, no compass to serve as guide, and no chart to tell us where we are.

Others are ready not only to welcome the change, seeing a new vitality and a fresh depth of concern in the emerging philosophy of Christian education, but also to go a step further to ask about changes that should be introduced to enable the Christian church to do its assigned task in the twentieth century.

Recent books in the field of Christian education deal with a myriad of subjects: the role of the Bible in our educational framework, theories of learning, education in the local church, surveys of the several schools of thought and the contributions which they have made, education theoretical and education practical—and a host of other general as well as more specific topics.

Within this context of transition, involving criticism, experimentation, restructuring, and reevaluation, Paul M. Lederach undertakes to think anew about the teaching ministry of the church. He speaks as a committed churchman in a denominational framework, the Mennonite Church. The issues to which he addresses himself and the concerns he expresses grow out of his own experience as educator, pastor, and administrator in the several areas of the denominational ministry.

Beginning with a survey of the scriptural basis for instruction, Lederach briefly traces the several steps in the development of an approach in Protestant religious education from the pioneer days of the American frontier to our own time, noting particularly how the Mennonites were influenced in the process. In the course of the survey an interesting phenomenon comes to light. With the coming of the Sunday school there was decided opposition to this kind of religious instruction from several Mennonite quarters. Now, 100 years later, the opposition against anything that would alter the Sunday school as it now functions is just as keen, and now as then, the arguments are as equally untenable.

Lederach's analysis of the educational program in our churches is long overdue. If Christian education is not an end in itself, then it is clear that the entire church program needs refurbishing. The teaching ministry is to undergird the congregation, and that ministry must fit our twentieth-century congregations—it is no longer the post-Civil War period to which we minister. Just as the early church did not allow herself to be fettered by rigid forms, so we too must be flexible, "responsive to needs, to situations, and to persons with gifts."

Striking out with boldness, Lederach speaks to the practical questions of cost, appropriate buildings, adequately trained personnel, and pertinent teaching materials. The lessons learned in the several projects of joint preparation and publication of graded materials (those of the Mennonite Church and the General Conference) need to be applied in every pertinent area, with further attention given to objectives, leadership, curriculum, and program. For the teaching ministry to be relevant there must be flexibility and involvement, and it is this to which the author calls our churches. He deserves to be heard.

Henry Poettcker, Th. D., *President*
Canadian Mennonite Bible College, Winnipeg

Contents

1

Teaching Among the People of God

Teaching in Ancient Israel

Both the Old Testament and the New Testament make clear the fact that teaching among God's people was always taken seriously. In ancient Israel teaching was for all persons across the life-span. There was great concern for teaching children. The prophets, the priests, and the wise men demonstrate the concern for teaching adults. Much of the Old Testament was written by men who were the teachers of the people.

Proverbs, a repository of Israel's educational insights, indicates that the object of education was insight or understanding. "The fear of the Lord," Proverbs 9:10 says, "is the beginning of wisdom, and the knowledge of the Holy One is insight." Teachers were known as "the wise." In Proverbs 15:7 we read, "The lips of the wise spread knowledge." Or, in Proverbs 13:14, "The teaching of the wise is a fountain of life, that one may avoid the snares of death."

Those taught were called "sons." "My son, if sinners entice you, do not consent" (Proverbs 1:10). Or, "And now, O sons, listen to me, and do not depart from the words of my mouth" (Proverbs 5:7). Later, in synagogue schools, students were called "sucklings of the house of their teachers."

In Israel the child was very important. The child was

considered a precious gift from the Lord, given to those who were deserving. This is expressed in Psalm 127:3-5, "Sons are a heritage from the Lord, the fruit of the womb a reward. . . . Happy is the man who has his quiver full of them!"

Where the child is considered important, in that society, education is also important. The Old Testament indicates that the most important function of parenthood was the rearing and training of children. Parents were to teach the wisdom of God that led to fearing God and to the life of righteousness. The life of righteousness was important because they believed it led to God's blessing with wealth and long life.

Among the Israelites, teaching had three overarching purposes.

1. The Israelites transmitted their historical heritage. Parents were responsible to root their child in that heritage. They did this by rehearsing the stories of God's redemptive acts. While telling the stories the parents relived the events and experienced anew God's saving activity. As they told the stories of bondage in Egypt, of deliverance through the Red Sea, and of entry into Canaan, children became aware of the roots of the people of whom they were a part.

In addition to the stories, parents also capitalized on the child's natural curiosity. When Israel crossed the Jordan (Joshua 4:20-22), large stones were taken from the riverbed and piled on the shore. Why was this done? To teach children. When children asked, "What do these stones mean?" an opportunity was provided to tell again what God had done for Israel. The Passover aroused the curiosity of children. When families observed the ceremonies, children asked, "What does this mean?" In response, parents would rehearse the story of deliverance.

2. The Israelites gave instruction in ethical conduct. In

Genesis 18:17-19, the Lord said concerning Abraham, "Shall I hide from Abraham what I am about to do, seeing that Abraham shall become a great and mighty nation, and all the nations of the earth shall bless themselves by him? No, for I have chosen him, that he may charge his children and his household after him to keep the way of the Lord by doing righteousness and justice; so that the Lord may bring to Abraham what he has promised him." God chose Abraham because he would teach the righteousness that God demands.

In Leviticus 19:2, the Lord said to Moses, "Say to all the congregation of the people of Israel, You shall be holy; for I the Lord your God am holy." On the basis of God's holiness follows a long list of instructions for holiness or ethical living among God's people. There was to be reverence for parents. "Every one of you shall revere his mother and his father" (verse 3). There was to be care and concern for the poor. "When you reap the harvest . . . you shall not reap your field to its very border" (verse 9). Let that along the border for the poor. There was to be no stealing, no false deals, no lying. Verse 11. There was to be no oppressing of one's neighbor, or withholding wages, or robbery. Verse 13. There was to be concern for the handicapped. Verse 14. In Israel, ethical conduct and concern for social justice grew out of their knowledge of the holiness of God. It was a matter of obedience to God's revelation rather than a striving toward ideals.

3. The Israelites taught practical conduct and common trades. The little things that make life go smoothly were emphasized. They told children how to relate to peers and to superiors. Children were told how to keep out of trouble. They were taught good manners and sensible sex conduct. Parents taught children to do simple tasks of the household. Boys were taught to pasture sheep and to work in the

fields. Girls were taught to bake, spin, and to weave. Artistic training was not overlooked. Children were taught to dance and to play musical instruments. Teaching methods were described in Isaiah 28:9, 10, "precept upon precept, line upon line." In other words, a little at a time.

Israelites were interested in teaching adults. One of the first large-scale adult education programs in history was carried on after the Exile by Ezra and Nehemiah in their great street school. Nehemiah 8.

It is interesting to reflect on Jewish education, especially on what it lacked and what it contained. Obviously, there was little scientific material in their teaching. Hebrew culture was prescientific. The Israelites knew little about physics, chemistry, biology, physiology, and the other natural sciences we know today. But they knew many practical things! They were familiar with the skills necessary for constructing buildings. They understood simple mining and metal work. However, their schools apparently did not teach these skills. They had no schools of music, of architecture, of sculpture, or of painting. They did not cultivate the arts in the manner of the Greeks and Romans.

The basic content in Jewish teaching, especially in the later times, was the Scripture. They believed that God inspired the Scriptures and thus they were a perfect repository of truth. They believed that the Scriptures contained all that was necessary for the welfare and happiness of men now and in the life to come. This was in contrast to Greek views of knowledge. The tendency of Greek thought, as of Roman, was to emphasize human capabilities. The Greeks and Romans believed that man's mind itself discovered truth. Consequently, they stressed the development of human reasoning which led to the study of sciences and to the abstract disciplines of philosophy. The Hebrews, on the other hand, believed that all truth comes from God, that God is Creator, the Judge, the Redeemer, and that He reveals whatever is necessary for man and his welfare. So Hebrew education revolved around concepts of God and man. Education had to do with moral and spiritual life because, in their view, man's health, prosperity, and well-being were dependent upon a satisfactory relationship with God. [1]

Jesus as Teacher

It would be a helpful endeavor to review here the life of Jesus and His work as a teacher. This has been done many times. Many helpful volumes are available. Today there may be tendencies to credit Jesus with teaching ability and skills that probably He Himself would have been surprised to hear about. Too often persons go to the Gospel records to support some current educational notion. For example, someone notes that Jesus spoke to a woman at a well. He notes further that the woman was thirsty and that Jesus began the conversation requesting a cup of water. The Christian educator reads back into this account his notions about readiness, beginning where people are, etc. Perhaps we do Jesus little service by reading into what He did our current ideas about how people learn or about how best to teach. To picture Jesus as a completely successful teacher may not do justice to Him or the records. In fact, Jesus Himself would likely have been first to admit some problems as a teacher. At times He just didn't get through to His pupils. In Mark, for example, He tried three times to teach the same lesson but with little apparent success. The first attempt occurred near Caesarea Philippi. Jesus taught that He was going to go to Jerusalem, suffer, die, and on the third day rise again. The group paid little attention. Only Peter responded to the effect, "Look, this isn't the way things should go!" He rebuked Jesus for such talk. Peter wanted Jesus to go to Jerusalem but not that way. Jesus replied that Peter was not reflecting God's way, and more, He said that persons can't follow Him unless they are ready to take up the cross and be the same kind of revolutionary. Mark 8:31-38.

Jesus attempted to teach the same lesson a second time. Mark 9:30-32. This time the disciples were afraid to ask questions. Instead, they discussed matters among themselves—but not the issues He raised. When they arrived in Capernaum, Jesus asked, "What were you discussing on the way?" He found out it wasn't the lesson! They were arguing who was the greatest. Jesus was trying to teach the heart of the gospel, but the class didn't respond to it, and they didn't discuss it. They had a completely different agenda.

Jesus attempted to teach the lesson a third time on the road to Jerusalem. Mark 10:32-45. He was preparing them for Jerusalem. But what happened? Did anyone listen or learn? Before He could finish, James and John came with a request, "Teacher, we want You to do for us whatever we ask of You." Jesus replied, "What do you want?" They said, "Well, one of us would like to be on Your right hand and the other on Your left hand in Your glory." This appears to be about as frustrating a situation as a teacher can find—a group that completely ignores what is being taught.

We should not read into Jesus' teaching our methods nor our notions of success, or of failure. Obviously, Jesus was an effective teacher and yet He had problems as a teacher.

Teaching in the Early Church

Early Christians placed a strong emphasis on teaching. The picture in Acts 2:42 is a significant one: "They devoted themselves to the apostles' teaching and fellowship, to the breaking of bread and the prayers." What inspired the spiritual and moral life of the believer was no longer the law recited in the synagogue service. Now it was the living Christ with whom they fellowshiped through the apostolic teaching, through the breaking of bread, and through prayers.

In the early church, Christian education was very flexible. Teaching was done as the situation demanded. Their program was based on persons rather than structures. Fortunately, we can't go to the New Testament to find structures or to defend the ones we have. The early church did not allow herself to get bound down to fixed forms as we do. They were flexible, responsive to needs, to situations, and to persons with gifts.

In 1 Corinthians 12:27-31, Paul wrote about the gifts God appointed in the church, "first apostles, second prophets, third teachers, then workers of miracles, then healers, helpers, administrators, speakers in various kinds of tongues." Apostles came first because it was they who founded the church by their testimony to the risen Christ. Prophets were inspired preachers who proclaimed the gospel in clear and comprehensible language, unlike those who spoke in tongues. Teachers interpreted the Christian message. They showed its relation to the Old Testament, and brought to light all of its riches. In other words, prophets and teachers explained to believers and helped them apply to their lives and circumstances the message of salvation that was brought by the apostles.

In Ephesians 4, Paul wrote about equipping saints for the work of ministry. This was an overarching objective of the teaching ministry. This is different from current practices which seem to have overarching objectives of keeping the teaching agencies going—scheduled, staffed, and growing.

What was taught in the early church? The New Testament provides a rather complete picture of teaching content.[2] This content could be divided into six areas:

1. Early Christians interpreted and expounded the Old Testament in the light of the Christ event. It was the Bible of the early church. Paul reasoned from the Scriptures. Jesus, before His ascension, went through "all the scriptures" (Luke 24:27) to demonstrate how they pointed toward Him. When Philip ministered to the Ethiopian (Acts 8:26-39), he began with Isaiah to tell the good news of Jesus. Today the Old Testament is of fundamental importance. It presents God, not as an abstraction, but as One who acts in history. It understands the corporate nature of the people of God. Through its prophets God reveals His will for social justice. He gives warnings and signs. It shows that judgment follows rebellion, but even then God forgives and restores. The Old Testament makes it clear why Christ came.

2. Early Christians rehearsed and explored the meaning of the words of Jesus. When Paul met with the Ephesian elders (Acts 20:17-38), he quoted one of Jesus' sayings, "It is more blessed to give than to receive." Today there is a tendency to overlook both the life of Jesus and His sayings while emphasizing the cross, resurrection, and His return. Perhaps the creeds have contributed to this. In the Apostolic Creed, for example, the life of Jesus is ignored: "Born of the Virgin Mary, crucified under Pontius Pilate." This is unfortunate. Today, in addition to the belief that Jesus reveals God to man, we need to be reminded that Jesus also reveals God's intention for man.

We must, like the early church, deal with His sayings. This is illustrated by Paul who constantly used or referred to the words of Jesus. 1 Thessalonians 5 is filled with words and phrases used by Jesus. Note the italicized words. Paul wrote, "But as to the times and the seasons, brethren, you have no need to have anything written to you. For you yourselves know well that the day of the Lord will come like a *thief in the night*. When people say, 'There is peace and security,' then sudden destruction will come upon them as *travail comes upon a woman with child*, and there will be no escape." The sayings of Jesus alluded to here are from Matthew 24:43, 45 and John 16:21. Paul continued, "But you are not in darkness, brethren, for that day to surprise you like a thief. For you are all *sons of light* [in Luke 16:8, Jesus referred to sons of light and sons of darkness] and sons of the day; we are not of the night or of darkness. So then let us not sleep, as others do, but let us keep awake and be sober." This echoes the words of Jesus concerning servants waiting for their Lord. Mark 13:33-37; Luke 21:34-36.

1 Timothy 5:17 provides another example: "Let the elders who rule well be considered worthy of double honor, especially those who labor in preaching and teaching; for the scripture says, 'You shall not muzzle an ox when it is treading out the grain,' and, 'The laborer deserves his wages.'" The first quotation is from Deuteronomy 25:4. The second is a direct quotation from Jesus. When Jesus sent out the seventy, He told them, "The laborer deserves his wages" (Luke 10:7). Early Christians held the words of Jesus as precious. They tried to discern their meaning and to apply them to daily situations.

3. Early Christians taught doctrine. That doctrine was taught is evidenced by the compact statements of faith, which crystallize the central emphases of the gospel. Many are found in Paul's epistles. These short, pithy generalizations helped the unlearned have a repository of doctrine that they could comprehend, meditate upon, and share. In 1 Timothy 2:5, 6 is one of these: "For there is one God,

and there is one mediator between God and men, the man Christ Jesus, who gave himself as a ransom for all." In Ephesians 4:4 f. is another, "There is one body and one Spirit, just as you were called to the one hope that belongs to your call, one Lord, one faith, one baptism, one God and Father of us all, who is above all and through all and in all." These doctrinal crystallizations were for adults so that they could be "doing business" with the Christian message.

4. Early Christians taught how to confess one's faith in the world. There was much emphasis on helping people make the "good confession" by word and deed as Jesus made the "good confession." 1 Timothy 6:13, 14. Peter made the "good confession," "You are the Christ" (Matthew 16:16). In the New Testament there is repeated emphasis upon the central confession, "Jesus is Lord." John 9:22; 12:42; Romans 10:9; 1 Corinthians 12:3; Philippians 2:11. The early church not only helped adults crystallize and understand the doctrines; it also helped them to confess wherever they were, "Jesus is Lord." This would be an exciting teaching ministry today—to help persons become knowledgeable doctrinally and to help them make the great confession, "Jesus is Lord," in all of life.

5. Early Christians taught ethics and morality. Evidences of this are on every hand. The epistles are filled with catalogs of virtues and vices. They are found in Galatians 5:19-23; Ephesians 4:19—5:8; Colossians 3:5-14; 1 Timothy 1:9-11; 4:12; 6:11; 2 Timothy 2:22; 3:2-5, 10, and Titus 3:3 f. As an illustration, note Colossians 3:5-11. First, the vices: "Put to death therefore what is earthly in you: immorality, impurity, passion, evil desire, and covetousness, which is idolatry. On account of these the wrath of God is coming. In these you once walked, when you lived in them. But now put them all away: anger, wrath, malice,

slander, and foul talk from your mouth. Do not lie to one another, seeing that you have put off the old nature with its practices and have put on the new nature, which is being renewed in knowledge after the image of its creator." Then the virtues: "Put on then, as God's chosen ones, holy and beloved, compassion, kindness, lowliness, meekness, and patience, forbearing one another and, if one has a complaint against another, forgiving each other; as the Lord has forgiven you, so you also must forgive. And above all these put on love, which binds everything together in perfect harmony."

Such passages are more than catalogs of sin and virtues. They are outlines for significant studies. These studies were specific; each word brings to the surface a whole range of insights and behavior. The New Testament is clear that the early church spent a good deal of time dealing with questions of morality. Today, we must ask, When are issues like these dealt with in our congregation? In Sunday school? In those ten verses adults go over so lightly each Sunday in the Uniform Series?

6. Early Christians prepared persons to participate in the gathered life of the congregation. In this area, practical problems of congregational life were dealt with. For example, when should widows be enlisted in the relief fund? 1 Timothy 5:3-17. How should leaders be selected in the congregation? 1 Timothy 3:1-12; Titus 1:5-9. What about financial support of church leaders? 1 Corinthians 9. How should various services be conducted? 1 Corinthians 11.

In the centuries following the apostles, the church continued to teach. There was the period of the "catechumenate." This had an emphasis on ethical teaching since the candidate for baptism had to know the kind of life to which he was committing himself. It had very little doctrinal content; the Creed, the Lord's Prayer, information about the baptism and communion seemed to be the extent of it. As years rolled by, teaching seemed to wither on the vine. By the fifth century, the catechumenate passed out of the picture. Late in the eighth century when Charlemagne attempted to bring reforms, he stimulated instruction in three areas: the Lord's Prayer, the Creed, and certain specified sins. [3] From then on, teaching seemed to move from preaching to symbolism found in buildings and in the worship services. One gets the feeling that Christian teaching became an almost unknown entity until the Reformation.

Teaching Among Anabaptists

Here it is impossible to deal with the rise of the teaching ministry in the Reformation, except to fasten on a few facets of the Anabaptist fringe.

An interesting document growing out of the Anabaptist movement concerns infant dedication found in Pilgram Marpeck's confession of 1531.

With respect to young children, in the presence of the Lord, the name of the child is to be given in the congregation and God is to be faithfully praised for this creature. His fatherly goodness is to be thanked and lauded, that through Christ Jesus our Lord and Savior He has also shown Himself merciful to even the unknowing or innocent creatures and without distinction taken them under His hand and promised them the kingdom of God. Thus we are obliged not only occasionally but at all times to be thankful for all of His good deeds and alongside of it to pray for everyone including for the child, that in the future it may along with us share God's gracious will according to the freedom of the Spirit and the word of Christ. The parents are to be charged to purify their conscience concerning the child, to do everything under their power to train it unto the glory and praise of God and to commit it to God until such time when it will be recognized what God will work in him whether to faith or unfaith.

Concerning this rite, William Klassen notes that the service is, first of all, one of thanksgiving and praise, particularly for the fact that God's mercy and Christ's work of salvation extend to this little child. Second, there is a petition for everyone in the church, but also for the child that it may begin to participate in the gracious will of God to the congregation and thus find freedom for its life. Third, parents are charged to do what their consciences allow; to do their share but in the final analysis to commit their child unto the grace and care of God. Fourth, the family is recognized as a unit in the congregation and this high point in its experience becomes a part of the public festivities of the church.

Anabaptists gathered for teaching and admonition. It is also clear that they considered the home as a center for Christian teaching. Around 1670 in Holland the interest of parents in instructing their children decreased, and then the church took over the task of religious education. At that time, church boards in many congregations ordered their ministers to instruct the children, but many ministers thought this was wrong. In 1692, E. A. van Dooregeest wrote that this was not the task of the preacher, but that the parents should educate their children in the teaching and admonition of the Lord. As late as 1760 K. de Vries, a minister in Amsterdam, warned from the pulpit against the religious teaching of the children by the ministers. [4]

Deeply ingrained in the Mennonite Church from early days is the idea that Christian teaching is a function of the home. The route to the child was this: In the congregation there was preaching. As adults came to faith, they entered the church. Through continuing instruction and preaching, parents received the necessary background to provide Christian teaching for their children. This also is how Christian education was done in the early church. In Ephesians

6:4, fathers were instructed to bring up their children in the "discipline and instruction of the Lord." Increasingly parental responsibility must be emphasized again.

From these paragraphs a few observations could be made:

1. The teaching ministry among the people of God through the ages has related to the total life and work of the people. The teaching ministry has not been some sort of parallel work like "Sunday school *and* church." It has been at the very heart of the church's life and work.

2. The teaching ministry must be consistent with the nature of the church, it must transmit the faith of the people of God, and undergird them in fulfilling their mission.

3. The teaching ministry was not an end in itself. It always filled the servant role, serving persons rather than using them, preparing persons for ministry to which God calls.

4. Through the ages the quality of worship, fellowship, and service is related to the seriousness with which the people of God undertook the teaching ministry.

5. The teaching ministry is for all persons among the people of God across the life-span. It is a lifelong process.

Discussion Questions

1. In what ways did the Israelites instruct their children and what was the basic content of the Jewish teaching?

2. Why should we exercise care in drawing "lessons" from the methods Jesus used in His teaching?

3. In the early church what did the Christians teach one another?

4. How was Christian teaching looked upon by the Anabaptists during the Reformation?

5. Is it possible today for parents to be made primarily responsible for the Christian education of their children?

6. Since the church survived 1800 years without the Sunday school, would the church survive today without it?

7. When are questions of ethics and morality dealt with in your congregation?

1. S. G. McCasland, *Interpreter's Dictionary of the Bible,* Vol. 2, p. 34.

2. I am indebted to Ian A. Muirhead, *Education in the New Testament,* for many of the ideas in this section.

3. L. J. Sherrill, *The Rise of Christian Education,* pp. 196, 231.

4. "Catechism," *Mennonite Encyclopedia,* Vol. 1, p. 529.

2

Development of the Present Strategy

Charles Merrill Smith in *How to Become a Bishop Without Being Religious* discusses, with tongue in cheek, the
young pastor's confrontation with the typical educational
program.

Every church, as you know, has attached to it a number of
subsidiary organizations. Most important of these is the Sunday
School. While the church has been going now for some two thou-
sand years, the Sunday School has been around only about two
hundred years. Amazingly, in those two hundred years, it has
nearly caught up with the church in size, organizational loyalty,
and the reverence with which its zealots treat it. It is, in fact, a
separate religious institution masquerading as a part of your
church but actually in direct competition with the church. It has
its own organizational structure, its own budget, its own promotional program, its own worship services. Therefore many of its
adherents consider it an adequate substitute for the church, as
witness the big procession heading for home as soon as Sunday
School is dismissed. These people never think of attending church.
They get their weekly dose of religion in Sunday School.

You may be distressed at this state of affairs in your early
pastorates, but the wisest course for you to follow is to learn to
live with it, because the situation will not change. Remember
that you are responsible for the Sunday School. You will have to
work with it. So we include two principles to keep in mind at
all times as you deal with it, which—if you observe them scru-
pulously—should enable you to stay out of trouble.

The first principle is that the Sunday School is a sacred cow, and thus should never be criticized, improved or tampered with in any way. The fury of a woman's scorn is a mild irritation compared with the animosity elicited from a good and faithful Sunday School superintendent to whom it is suggested that the S.S. could stand a little refurbishing. If you, his pastor, are so witless as to suggest it you will succeed only in mobilizing the entire Sunday School organization to a dedicated and unrelenting effort to oust you from the church. . . .

The second principle is that you must not confuse the function of the Sunday School with education. Admittedly the name "school" is misleading, and inexperienced pastors nearly always waste enormous amounts of time and effort trying to make of the S.S. a teaching enterprise before they discover that the Sunday School does not exist in order that pupils may learn anything. In fact, the genuinely superior Sunday Schools are those which impart the least factual information to their students. This apparent paradox is explained when you remember that S.S. teachers are volunteers, that they are dealing with material they know nothing about (and probably haven't even read), so whatever they do manage to teach is likely to be misinformation—which is worse than no information. . . .

You will be expected to visit these classes, and the average freshly minted seminary graduate is appalled at the theology dispensed in them. It ranges from fundamentalist pietism through salvation by thinking gorgeous thoughts, with both extremes frequently included in the same lesson by the same teacher, with no one bothered in the least by the inconsistencies.

The surest way to kill off a large, popular adult Sunday School class is to insist that it devote itself to serious study. Americans have, for a long time now, been told that if a group of people who know nothing whatever about a subject spend an hour or so pooling their ignorant and uninformed opinions the end product will be insights whose truth is beyond question and an occult wisdom unattainable by lesser methods. This is the faith in which the adult S.S. class is founded, and to destroy it is to destroy the institution. [1]

Smith's paragraphs are humorous, but the humor is in their reflection of a tragic situation. Could the same be written about Mennonite churches? How did our strategy develop?

The Early Days

Mennonites came to North America in the latter part of the 1600's and early 1700's. Since then Mennonite groups have come at different times, from different places, and have settled in many different communities in the United States and Canada. In the early days of the frontier, the church was loosely structured. In eastern Pennsylvania, the congregations gathered at the meetinghouse every two weeks for worship. Activities beyond the biweekly assembly were quite limited. The congregation was central. There were no parallel or competing teaching organizations. Teaching beyond the worship services was limited to a class to instruct persons anticipating baptism. Teaching children was seen as the responsibility of the family.

While the first two or three hymns were being sung, the ministers held a meeting in the "little room" to plan the services for the day. Such matters were seldom prearranged. Here they decided who would read the morning lesson and who would preach. This anteroom was used also as an instruction room for young men and women who intended to unite with the church. Only grown young people or young married folks were supposed to join this class. They received instruction every Sunday when there was preaching—usually every two weeks. The period of instruction began in April or May and continued until July or August when the young people were baptized. This was the only public religious instruction intended primarily for young people. Instruction was given entirely by the ministers in a private session that began an hour or more before time for services. After the congregation had sung several long hymns to very slow tunes, the young people would file in from the anteroom and take seats on the front bench. . . .

Services began between nine and ten and seldom closed as early as twelve. On the Sunday when the semiannual communion services were held, the meeting was not dismissed until about four o'clock in the afternoon.[2]

One reason for the lengthy communion service was the preaching of holy history. On these occasions, ministers traced God's redemptive activity from Genesis to Christ.

In colonial times the teaching ministry consisted of sermons and of instruction for persons anticipating baptism. The home carried the main burden for teaching children. The church undertook its work with children through the family. The family taught through family worship and the interaction of parents and children.

In 1849 a letter from Germany asked a family in Waterloo, Ontario, "Is family worship observed in all the families?" In answer, David Sherk wrote, "If you mean to ask, and I suppose you do, whether parents hold regularly social prayer at home with their families I must answer, that, so far as I know, there are but few who do this: though I would much rather see it otherwise, and be able in truth to give a different answer, if it were done in simplicity to the honor of God and not merely to be seen of men."[3]

In those days things were not ideal! Then, as now, there was the wish and the hope that there would be worship in the home. Then, as now, the practice was not universal in Christian homes.

One indication, however, of the seriousness with which homes took religious teaching was a tremendous publishing project undertaken before the Revolutionary War. This was the translation and publication of the *Martyrs Mirror*. When the flames of the French and Indian War were rising, Mennonite parents were concerned lest their sons be caught up in the militarism of the day. To counteract this, the Dutch book, *Martyrs Mirror*, which contained accounts of nonresistant martyrs, was translated from Dutch to German, printed and published in eastern Pennsylvania. This great volume was an important tool for the home to educate children in the nonresistant way.

Mennonite homes were not without literature to help in

religious instruction. In the decade after the Civil War, 1865-75, the average home would have these publications:[4] First, a Bible; more than likely the Froschauer Swiss Bible. This was the preferred version. Second, a hymnal; likely the *Ausbund,* which is still used among the Old Order Amish. As early as 1803, Mennonites in eastern Pennsylvania (Franconia Conference) published the hymnbook, *Zion's Harp.* In 1804 the Lancaster Conference also published one, the *Impartial Hymnbook* (which really meant undenominational hymnbook).

Many homes had theological writings. First among these would be the writings of Menno Simons. Dirk Philips' book, the *Enchiridion,* would also be available.

Many homes had a prayer book. *The Earnest Christian's Duty* was published as early as 1745. Some would have confessions of faith. More than likely many homes would have the *Dordrecht Confession of Faith,* 1632, or that of P. J. Twisck.

Catechisms would be available, either the long or shorter catechism of Gerrit Roosen or the *Waldeck Catechism,* which contained those 202 questions and answers.

Some homes had history books. There was an early Mennonite attempt to write Bible history in a strange book called, *The Wandering Soul.* Benjamin Eby published a brief church history and doctrine book. A few homes had books of sermons and theological monographs. Among the monographs would be one on baptism by Funk; one on repentance by Burkholder; one on the new birth by Godschalk; and one on nonresistance by Funk and Brenneman.

Whether the teaching ministry consisting of instruction classes for new members and home teaching provided an adequate educational base for that time is hard to assess.

The Coming of the Sunday School

The Sunday school had its rise in England around 1780. Robert Raikes, of Gloucester, is generally looked to as the founder of this movement. Some feel that Sunday schools reached North America as early as 1785. And some Mennonites, a little like some nations that are accused of changing history for their benefit, claim that the Mennonites had the first Sunday school near Harrisburg, Pennsylvania, around 1745. Whether this glorious claim can be supported is doubtful.

The Sunday school thrived in North America. By 1825 the American Sunday School Union was established. As early as 1830 this organization resolved to establish Sunday schools in every town in the Mississippi Valley. In 1834 it resolved to establish Sunday schools throughout the South. The American Sunday School Union was a vigorous organization. It planted Sunday schools throughout the frontier. But Sunday school changed radically when it moved from the inner city of England to the American wilderness. At first Sunday school, as Raikes conceived it, was a venture in social action. Raikes was concerned about city children who lacked opportunities to study and receive religious instruction. Furthermore, Raikes was deeply concerned about the quality of teaching. In fact, he paid the teachers to teach in his Sunday school. He wanted good teaching and competent teachers. He knew this had to be paid for, and he did! When Raikes died, little children were paid to sing at his funeral. They were given a "shilling and a plum cake."[5]

When Sunday school came to North America, it was changed from a tool for social action to a tool for evangelization. Instead of helping children in the inner city, it evangelized the frontier. As Sunday schools dotted the landscape, congregations of many denominations looked askance at the young, thriving institution. There were many reasons for this. The more conservative were scandalized by some of the activities Sunday school promoted such as picnics and other gimmicks to encourage attendance. For the most part, Sunday schools were opposed by denominational hierarchies who were threatened by the lay orientation of Sunday school structures. This was true in the Mennonite Church. In the archives is a letter from brethren opposing Sunday school because laymen were teaching. Teaching was to be in the hands of the ministry. These brethren opposed the Sunday school for many other reasons. Another was that it would take the Bible out of the public school! Another, it would take Bible teaching out of the home.

In the 1867 minutes of the Virginia Mennonite Conference is this:

The subject of Sunday school was brought up and spoken against. It was not thought best that we should send our children to Sunday school, in the way schools are conducted, neither in the way that we understand that some of our brethren in the West have them. We can have our Sunday schools in our houses. The Apostle Paul admonishes us to bring up our children in the nurture and admonition of the Lord.

These minutes, which were printed in the *Herald of Truth*, the denominational organ of the day, brought a response from a brother in Illinois, which was in the "West." Samuel Hirstein wrote:

How Sunday schools are conducted in other places I know not, but since we in the West are particularly referred to, we will inform the dear brethren in Virginia, and all others, how we conduct our Sunday school.

We open with singing and prayer, after which the children are divided into classes. The first class reads in the Testament by turns. [Was this the beginning of the round robin Sunday school teaching?] The passages of Scripture are explained, questions are asked, and exhortations are given. The children also commit

39

verses from the Scriptures to memory. The second class are those who still need instruction in reading. To this class also verses are given to commit to memory. The third class are those who cannot read at all. We also endeavor to advance each class. To my knowledge nothing disorderly has yet occurred, although we do not consider ourselves without fault, and should any one have observed anything out of place, we desire that they would tell us of our faults or give some scriptural reason to show us that we are in the wrong.

It is further said, "We can have our Sunday schools in our houses." The instruction of our children in our own houses, where it is observed, is one of the best virtues, but it is a certain truth that the lesson our Savior taught, especially to Peter and all the apostles, reaches further than our own houses.[6]

It wasn't long until Sunday schools were no longer separate. They moved closer to the congregation. In many communities active laymen worked in both the congregation and the community Sunday school. Soon Sunday school was brought inside the congregation. The General Conference Mennonite Church in eastern Pennsylvania was ahead of the Mennonite Church in adopting Sunday schools. The first permanent Sunday school in the Mennonite Church was founded in 1863 at West Liberty, Ohio.

Even though Sunday schools came into congregations, Charles Merrill Smith is quite correct when he observes that they were not absorbed by congregations. Today, in many congregations, Sunday school continues to have its own structures, its own budget, its own loyalties, and is still maintaining, at least verbally, that its main thrust is evangelism just as in the good old days on the frontier. Today we have to ask, What is the role of the Sunday school? And, Is it the locus of evangelism for the congregation?

As the Sunday school gained admittance, it brought along Sunday school conferences and conventions. It brought missionary awakening. It brought a strong em-

40

phasis on temperance. It also brought vigorous promotional programs, especially for increased attendance. The Sunday school went full circuit, from opposition to full support with slogans like, "Build the church through the Sunday school" or "Bigger Sunday Schools, Bigger Churches." Few people questioned these slogans or took time to ask whether this is indeed the way the church is enlarged. There is little evidence to demonstrate that this is the way to church growth. To say that 85 percent of the church members come out of the Sunday school blinds to the many persons who have attended Sunday school but have not decided for Christ and the church. In fact, one major denomination has made a careful study of this issue and found that "the number of years of Sunday school attendance was *not* a significant factor in increasing the likelihood of church membership as an adult."[7]

Youth Work and Sunday Evening Services

Our present strategy includes youth work and Sunday evening services. At one time these were closely related. In 1881, the movement, "Christian Endeavor," got under way. This too has been labeled as the "greatest movement" in religious education in the past century.[8] There were great Christian Endeavor Conventions. One in Philadelphia brought 6,500 delegates together. Later, in 1891, a convention in Minneapolis was attended by 14,000 people. Probably spinning off from this came the Sunday evening service which we called "Young People's Bible Meeting." Our churches did not adopt Christian Endeavor. In the decades past, emphasis was on young people. Now emphasis is on a Sunday evening service for all ages. Curriculum is prepared for this setting, an annual *Program Guide*. The Young People's Bible Meeting, however, illustrates again how a teaching agency came into congregations as a modified copy of a program extraneous to the congregation. The change in Sunday evening service did not mean that concern for youth was being dropped. This was picked up elsewhere, especially through the youth organizations (MYF or YPU) developed after World War II.

Summer Bible School

In 1901, Dr. Bouville, superintendent of the Baptist City Mission in New York City, was impressed one summer day, as he went to his office, that schools were closed, that mothers were working, and that children were left to the dangers of the street. He had a very interesting way of saying it:

> Idle children filling the streets,
> Idle churches dark and silent.
> Unemployed students on vacation,
> Idle vacation days and children's courts.

So he started a vacation Bible school.

Vacation Bible school began in the inner city and like Sunday school had both social and religious concerns. Daily vacation Bible schools spread rapidly. A National Vacation Bible School Committee was formed as early as 1907. In 1911 a Daily Vacation Bible School Association was formed. Denominations did not fight this new agency. They picked it up rapidly. Presbyterians were promoting it by 1913. In 1915 the Northern Baptists took it up. Soon it had spread throughout the church. Though the original intent of the vacation Bible school was to provide religious guidance and instruction for children roaming the hot streets of the inner city, it was easily adapted to the ways and purposes of rural congregations.

Summer Bible school received new impetus in Mennonite churches with the release of a curriculum in 1948. After this, growth was exceedingly rapid. Like other teaching agencies, summer Bible school grew up outside and came into the Mennonite Church. It demonstrated further the notion that Christian education was primarily for children.

Back in the decade of the forties, it was possible for many rural congregations to make Bible school a congregational project. Men left their farm work to help conduct Bible school. All children in the community were invited and did attend. Bible school was promoted with great vigor. Congregations worked hard. They used the whole building for vacation Bible school. They provided equipment. Many congregations had tables and blackboards for summer Bible school classes. They got them out for summer Bible school and then stored them away until next vacation Bible school. It was strange that the need for such equipment for the Sunday school was not perceived. In the early days, it was possible for men to be involved, to teach, to drive buses, etc., but gradually they dropped out of the picture. Then women took over. Today, women are no longer available as more and more are employed outside of the home.

In order to provide staff, congregations are changing from morning to evening sessions. Then, too, children are no longer free as they once were. Now there are Little Leagues and vacations. Camping and summer school compete for children's time. But we have our good curriculum, and we know that children ought to go through it. So congregations are turning to evening schools. In 1966, 47 percent of the summer Bible schools were held in the evening. This illustrates how a teaching agency can move from its original conceptualization.

It is not possible here to examine the coming of all the teaching agencies of our present strategy. One more should be noted, weekday Bible school. The church has looked with interest at this agency. The Lancaster Conference went so far as to prepare pupil and teacher materials for weekday Bible school. In 1954, it was agreed that after completing the graded Sunday school curriculum, work would begin on a weekday Bible school curriculum. Early in the sixties, a Weekday Bible School Counsel and Reference Committee was established. When the group began to work, it discovered that to create a weekday Bible school curriculum, a great deal more must be known about the total teaching ministry in order to see how a new curriculum would fit into the overall teaching of the congregation. When the group studied the stated objective for Sunday school, for Sunday evening service, for youth fellowship, for summer Bible school, for boys' clubs, and for girls' clubs, it found that when these objectives were put together, there was much overlap and the total was not comprehensive. Interestingly enough, each agency had the objective of evangelism. In studying the objectives it became clear that each agency viewed itself as a separate entity. It was not conceived within the context of the congregation. As a result each agency felt the need to carry many functions of the congregation. The notion that each agency could fill a unique function within the congregation, undergirding the congregation in its mission, was absent. Because the point of departure was the agency rather than the congregation, overlap and duplication were inevitable. In the process the need to integrate the role of the congregation and the significant and unique role of the agency was overlooked.

The studies for a weekday curriculum led to the conclusion that were a curriculum developed, it would be necessary to focus again on the congregation and not, as in the past, on one manifestation of the congregation's teaching ministry. No longer could each agency carry the overarching objectives of the congregation. Not every agency should be primarily "evangelistic" if the congregation is to function effectively.

Slowly the realization came that those in the teaching ministry must ask: What is the congregation? What is the task of the congregation? How is education done in a congregation? Answers to such questions, hopefully, could lead to understanding the unique contributions each agency could make to the overall purpose of the congregation.

For purposes of further discussion, these observations concerning our present strategy are offered:

1. Congregations recognize their responsibility for formal programs of education in the Christian faith. There is no doubt that teaching is an underlying and undergirding concern. This is illustrated by the many endeavors to borrow and to adopt structures for the teaching ministry from sources outside of the tradition.

2. These borrowings, for the most part, have been helpful, but they brought along some liabilities. For one thing the teaching ministry concentrated largely on children. This is made clear by current agencies and supporting curriculum materials. This emphasis on children has also in a measure been contrary to our commitment to a believer's church. Teaching children is not Christian education in its *primary* sense. In its primary sense it is educating those who have responded to Jesus Christ as Lord and Savior. Teaching children of families within the congregation is Christian education in a derived sense. In recent times, congregations have focused largely on Christian education in this derived sense, and not in the primary sense of teaching new disciples all that Jesus commanded.

3. Promotion has tended to develop similar programs in

each congregation. Because a teaching structure worked in one place, there was the feeling it should work in others. The primary questions, What is the purpose of the congregation in this place? and, How does this agency or structure contribute to the overall purpose here? were seldom asked. There is no end to what a congregation could add to its program now or in the future. Because one congregation has success with a boys' club all should have one, some promoters thought. Today, when one congregation succeeds with a coffee shop it is surprising to see how many congregations try to establish a coffee shop even though it may not fit the situation. There are places a coffee shop may help the church in its witness, but there is a special situation and there are persons with gifts and with a call. Obviously, much more is needed than a building that could contain a coffee shop.

In New York City one congregation is doing an excellent job through a sandwich shop with a pool table in a back room. This has provided many opportunities to contact and work with young people in the community. In the future, if things go as in the past, some will say, "We ought to have a sandwich shop with a pool table in our church." So they do. Then another congregation tries it. Eventually whenever educational wings are built, all will include sandwich shops with pool tables!

4. There is duplication of function from one teaching agency to another. This, likely, has resulted from failure to begin with the congregation because of the unspoken but very real misconception that Christian education is something parallel to the life of the congregation, separate but equal—the Sunday school *and* church syndrome.

5. Because of the fixing of variables in teaching agencies, flexibility is difficult. Though congregations are modi-

fying summer Bible school, they can scarcely conceive of a Sunday morning setting in which anything else is done except Sunday school as it has always been done. Even changing order so that Sunday school follows the church service sends a panic through some, and when Sunday school follows worship services, it is interesting to note how all the Sunday school parts stay intact. Sunday school still starts with a worship service, led by the superintendent, even though the congregation has just come through a worship experience. As a result, the Sunday school. hour stays chock-full of bits and pieces that take away from the class period. Such inflexibility keeps congregations from breaking out of ruts and making better use of time.

6. The teaching program has been vigorously promoted, largely in terms of attendance and structure. In some circles fieldmen are still preaching bigger and better Sunday schools. Their briefcases bulge with promotional gimmicks—all of course designed to have people "come" to Sunday school (March to Sunday School in March), with little emphasis on educating people to go into the world. In their briefcases are all kinds of colorful pamphlets, nifty little buttons, and answers to scores of questions nobody is asking. The "total program" doesn't ask about the purpose of the congregation; it merely tells a congregation to have Sunday school, summer Bible school, boys' clubs, girls' clubs, etc., and if it has all the blocks and all are stacked right it is doing Christian education—especially if each little block is geared to evangelism and is getting bigger and better. This approach is particularly in favor with independent religious publishers since each block provides a market for its product.

7. In the present strategy a congregation competes with itself for the time, abilities, and finances of persons to

keep the program going. Keeping things going becomes the end, though evangelism is the verbal rationale. In the midst of this complexity is the pastor, bewildered and overworked trying to satisfy jurisdictional disputes, trying to see that staff is available, and trying to iron out the calendar.

8. The present strategy is more concerned with structures than with the issues the church should be dealing with in the world. It is amazing how much time is spent on organizing this department and that, organizing this club and that fellowship. But who in the congregation is taking time to see what is being taught in each setting? What issues are being dealt with and how? And more, What are people learning? As long as the teaching ministry is composed of agencies, somewhat independent or apart, no one feels constrained to keep the whole in view. Each agency selects its own curriculum. Whether material comes from an independent religious publisher or from one's denominational house is a secondary issue when Christian education is seen as separate from the congregation and with its own structures. However, once the teaching ministry is seen at the very heart of the life of the congregation, then it becomes clear that whatever is taught must undergird the commitment and mission of the congregation. For too long structures and facilities have been emphasized without insisting that congregations ask, What are we going to teach this year? Even when denominational materials are used, this question must be asked; and when the Sunday school theme is Redemption, or Church, or Discipleship, pastors and teachers should work through these great themes together on a sound theological level.

In addition to structures, buildings also have been emphasized—buildings that will allow congregations to do

Christian education as usual, meeting simultaneously on Sunday morning, and letting a giant building stand idle during the week. The possibility of during-the-week sessions, with longer class periods, with professional teachers, has not been explored by very many persons.⁹ It is much easier to plan a building hoping it will improve teaching rather than to invest in persons to help the teaching ministry.

9. The present strategy requires a proliferation of teaching materials. Each agency calls for some sort of curriculum material to keep going. When materials are produced for an agency, there is the temptation to design them to keep the agency going rather than to undergird in a unique way the congregation's mission. Furthermore, content is duplicated. Since Mennonites believe the Bible is important, teachers in each agency insist that portions of the Bible must be in every piece. The result is that children study the same stories time and time again as they grow through the curricula prepared for various agencies.

10. The present strategy leads people to believe that being involved in and keeping the teaching structures going is Christian service. To a limited extent this is true. Of greater importance is defining Christian service as the life one lives at home, on the job, and in the neighborhood as a servant and witness for Jesus Christ. Too often keeping the internal congregation structures intact seals off the Christian from making worthwhile contributions in the community as night after night he sits in church committees.

Clearly we are at a point of reevaluation of our educational enterprise. Someone has observed that rearrangement of priorities and structural reorganization in the light of the mission and situation of the congregation are the medicines needed now. If such reevaluation results in institutional death, there is the likelihood of rebirth—which is far better than death by default.

Discussion Questions

1. To what extent is the quotation from Charles Merrill Smith at the beginning of this chapter true in your Sunday school?

2. When the Sunday school was brought to America, what changes took place in its function and emphasis?

3. How did it happen that we have come to think of Sunday school and church as two separate entities? Why has the emphasis in Christian education been almost exclusively on teaching children? In the teaching ministry when do persons move from "milk" to "meat"?

4. What dangers are there in emphasizing structure and attendance in Christian education programs?

5. Should the home cooperate with the congregation in the Christian education of children or should the congregation cooperate with the home in this task?

6. What is your understanding of Christian service and how does one prepare persons for it?

1. Charles Merrill Smith, *How to Become a Bishop Without Being Religious,* pp. 116-19.

2. John Umble, "Seventy Years of Progress in Sunday School Work Among the Mennonites of the Middle West," *Mennonite Quarterly Review,* October 1934, p. 168.

3. *Herald of Truth,* III (April 1866), p. 31.

4. For a more complete listing see J. C. Wenger, *The Church Nurtures Faith,* pp. 20-22.

5. William C. Seitz, "Robert Raikes," *Westminster Dictionary of Christian Education,* p. 552.

6. *Herald of Truth,* V (March 1868), p. 39.

7. William J. Millard, Jr., "Sunday School Training and Church Membership," *Religious Education,* November-December, 1964 (LIX-6), p. 502.

8. Clarence Benson, *A Popular History of Christian Education,* p. 206.

9. See Wesner Fallow, *Church Education for Tomorrow,* which suggests in depth, during-the-week study for all age-groups with professional teachers.

3

Today's Crisis

To reevaluate, to take a fresh look at what is being
done in the church, is always in order. In fact, this is
constantly necessary. Reformation must take place contin-
ually. Harold S. Bender has pointed out:

"The real life of the church as a human society is historically
and sociologically conditioned. The forms of organization and expression which now operate in the general church, that is, the
divided church, have been formed by human action and interaction and become embedded in human tradition, many of them
with no malicious purpose or schismatic intent. The constant
danger is that we absolutize these human realities. Expressions
of the life of the past tend to become so traditional, and thus so
hardened and rigid, that they block the flow of life in the body
of Christ from member to member and prevent the free action
of the Spirit in leading the church in various times and places
into creative new action and unity. [1]

Dr. Bender also wrote:

The church is always in danger of resisting the Holy Spirit.
. . . The gravest dangers here are two: (1) that the traditions of
the past may stifle the voice of the Spirit today; or (2) that leaders may seek to hold power in their own hands, and resist the
Spirit moving in others in the church. In either case, the result
is the same. Where God would lead forward and upward, or
would cleanse and purge, men resist. They resist opening themselves to new light; they refuse to respond to calls for new work;
they resist change; hallowed traditions are given unwarranted

religious sanction or even presumed scriptural endorsement; culture is confused with faith; commandments of men are made into commandments of God; institutions and administrators reject legitimate criticism, the brotherly address. [2]

It is imperative that the teaching ministry be reexamined. That there is a crisis, is dawning upon many persons. The extent of it is not clear, but symptoms are becoming clear. At least ten facets of the crisis are easily identified. They are listed, not in order of importance, but for consideration, for reaction, and for acceptance or rejection.

Recently I spent a weekend with nearly ninety Christian education leaders from a group of five churches. In the first session I said, "I have heard it said that the educational program in our congregations is in a crisis. Do you have evidence that this might be the case?" That was all that was needed. The group began to list one evidence after another. Members could hardly wait until others stopped talking so that they could elaborate upon other aspects of the crisis.

Today church members must be free to speak about the crisis as they see it, and in the context of the brotherhood try to discern ways to go. These ten facets of the crisis are listed to encourage conversations.

1. Congregations seem unaware of the new situation which calls for new forms in the teaching ministry. An evidence of this is the fact that Sunday school continues as the main pillar in the church's educational ministry, even though the situation which made it a viable option 100 years ago no longer exists. One hundred years ago, the church had at least two options open for its teaching ministry. It could promote parochial schools, or it could adopt the Sunday school.

Promoting parochial schools was a real option for Mennonites, since they had a long history in Mennonite communities. Anyone traveling in eastern Pennsylvania can still see next to many of the meetinghouses the small schoolhouses. The school was intertwined with the church's life. In fact, *School-Management*, the first book on pedagogy published in the colonies, was written by the Mennonite schoolmaster, Christopher Dock (in 1750), who came to North America through the port of Philadelphia and settled along Skippack Creek. He taught school in Skippack and later in Salford.

After the Civil War, the Sunday school was a viable option for the church's teaching ministry. [3] As noted earlier, when the Sunday school came to the North American frontier, it became an evangelizing institution. Even though parochial schools were in our tradition, the churches moved away from them because communities were largely Protestant and the public schools were doing the job Protestants wanted done. The public schools were the carriers of Protestant morality. They taught the Bible. This is quickly seen in a perusal of textbooks of the day. They were filled with quotations from the Bible. They emphasized the importance of work and showed the dire end of the slothful. They taught honesty and frugality.

The church saw that through the Sunday school it could do what was not being done in the public school, the teaching of sectarian or denominational specifics. For example, the merits of pouring or of immersion as the mode of baptism could not be argued in the public school. The main job was being done in the public school. The secondary, but equally important sectarian teaching could be done on a one-hour-a-week basis. Thus, the Sunday school was accepted by the church, but as a lean-to to the main structure, the public school. Mennonites were involved in this marriage as much as anyone else. Sunday schools were opposed until it was seen as a device to teach sectarian or cultural concerns. In some places Sunday school gained acceptance by teaching the German language. But the sectarian emphases won the day. Persons that opposed Sunday schools said, "You have no safe books. If you get books from other publishing houses, you will lead the people away with strange doctrine. So as soon as you get books from our own publishing houses teaching our own doctrines, you may have Sunday school. [4] That the public school was doing what many Mennonites wanted done is illustrated by some opposers of Sunday school. These men saw that if Sunday school were adopted by the church, this would lead to taking the Bible out of the public school. In fact, a letter listing many reasons why the Sunday school is wrong included this:

We object to it because it was instrumental to a great extent in banishing the Bible and Testament from weekday schools, thus giving Satan a greater scope of ground on weekdays and perhaps by a corrupt Sabbath school system on Sunday also. [5]

With teaching denominational concerns in view, the church was justified in spending only one hour a week in the endeavor, since the main work was being done in the home and in the public school. Today, public schools are no longer the carriers of Protestant morality. Bible reading and prayer, recently removed from the public school, were the last vestiges of that day, a century ago, when public schools taught the Bible and Puritan ethics. Yet the church has not awakened to the new situation. And strangely enough those most vigorous today in protesting the removal of prayer and Bible reading are also the persons that are the most vigorous in promoting the one-hour-per-week educational approach. Somehow, Christians are not alert to the new situation. It is not a matter of doing away with the Sunday school. It is a matter of frankly facing the fact that Sunday school just can't carry the freight. Something vastly more than the Sunday school is needed, something that really reflects the situation—the changes in home life, the impact of the media of mass communication, and the nationalistic, secular impact of public schools. Thus the crisis. We are perpetuating as the backbone of our teaching program a form that had significance in post-Civil War days as an adjunct of the public school. This form, now sacred for many, is keeping them from honestly facing the new situation and seeking new solutions.

2. Congregations provide inadequate time for the teaching ministry. No matter how well the church's educational goals may be stated, is it possible to accomplish them in a one-hour-per-week program? In a recent survey it was found that the average teaching time for a Protestant Sunday school class is twenty-nine minutes. Another denomination, which has just completed a study of its church school teachers, found that the average class period extends from thirty-six to forty minutes. When the Mennonite graded Sunday school curriculum was developed, materials for a thirty-minute class period were prepared. What can be done in thirty minutes? How seriously is the teaching ministry taken if this is all the time allotted?

It is interesting to note the teaching ministry that is being carried on in various Jewish communities. Their program staggers the imagination of the average Protestant. A rabbi explained it this way. When the present generation of middle-aged Jews came to the United States with their parents, they wanted, above everything else, to be assimilated into the American way of life. They rejected the ways of their parents along with their parents' religion. They wanted to be identified as Americans. All of a sudden, these people, who are now parents, became aware that their children are unfamiliar with the Jewish tradition and heritage. They lack a sense of identity. Consequently, these parents have undertaken a vigorous educational program for their children. Of what does it consist? The parents are seeing to it that their children get to the synagogue during the week for religious education. These children go to the synagogue six hours each week—two hours a day, for three days. They are taught Jewish history, Jewish ceremonies, and the Hebrew language. That this is being taken seriously is indicated by the fact that directors of these schools are being paid up to $15,000 a year. Clearly, when parents are committed to an educational ministry, when they see the urgency of it, things can be done.

Back to the short class periods. A manager of a steel mill in Calcutta visited in one of our North American churches. Even though a Hindu, he was interested in attending a church service, and a Sunday school class. The Sunday he visited, things went as usual. The class was together for forty-five minutes. Just as the group got to the point in the discussion where a decision should have been made, the bell rang. And like Pavlov's dogs (they salivate when the bell rings) the class got up and walked out. On the way from class the Indian said to one of the class members, "You know what you people should do? You should have class every other Sunday and then have two hours for discussion." A Hindu from Calcutta, who had not participated in a Sunday school class before, puts his finger right on the problem in the first visit.

3. Congregations provide inadequate financing for the teaching ministry. True, the church must operate on donated funds. There is no way around that system. But many congregations fail to see the importance of giving for teaching. "Missions" is the word that stirs people to give. What are congregations willing to pay for teaching? They

won't pay teachers. And lesson helps—they want to keep them as inexpensive as possible—in the area of 28-29¢ per quarter. If denominational prices go higher, many congregations rush to independent publishers where materials can be secured at less cost. The point is, congregations are ready to spend about 2¢ per week for curriculum for adults! An amazing amount! For children, denominational publishers have to keep pupil books around 40¢ per quarter, which is approximately 3¢ per week. If teacher's manuals go above $1.50 or $2.00 a year, it seems the sky falls in for many.

What kind of educational program is wanted if curriculum materials have to be based on pennies per week? Perhaps the 2¢ per week is a parable of the triviality of the church's teaching endeavor. The penny economy is another of the Civil War hangovers. Back in those days, they even sang about listening to pennies dropping. Apparently many congregations have not moved beyond this.

Another aspect of the problem is the way money is placed in buildings rather than in people. Is the best approach to Christian education the simultaneous one, when on Sunday morning everyone across the life-span meets for thirty to forty minutes? Should enormous buildings be erected for this kind of operation? Might it be better to use these funds to hire competent teachers—those who could teach various groups during the week (like our Jewish friends)? Actually interest from an $80,000 mortgage could pay a good portion of the salary of a person to teach various groups in the congregation, or it could be used to help staff members secure additional training and preparation. [6] This suggests the next facet of the crisis.

4. Congregations rely on a good-intentioned but often untrained, volunteer teaching staff. This crisis is evident in many ways. For example, when church curriculum mate-

rials are compared with those used in public schools, there is a wide gap in range of interest and of difficulty. Compare a junior high's Sunday school lesson help with his science, history, or mathematics text. The problem is not that Sunday school curricula cannot be produced on this level. The problem is that few churches would have teachers capable of handling it! The cry of teachers now is, Materials are too difficult; too much time is required to prepare. Make the materials easier. Easier for whom? It seems that what is asked for is material that an untrained teaching staff can use rather than materials which will assist the child to learn to the full extent of his capability. How can congregations upgrade the teaching staff? Perhaps children abhor Sunday school because of the flat, simple, repetitious experiences they endure because of the low capability of the teaching staff and the low interest level of curriculum material such staffs require.

5. Congregations have settled on inadequate purposes for the teaching ministry. Some congregations still use gimmicks and repeat slogans to increase attendance, for example, not realizing that the important thing is what happens to people when they get there. What is the difference between the educational ministry of the church and that of the public school? [7] This is a fairly difficult question. Involved is the matter of folk religion. The public school does a job of transmitting the national mythology which some say is Christian. The public school, however, wants to make the child a good citizen. It wants to make him a "democratic" citizen who will support the state whether right or wrong. The child is fed stories of George Washington and Lincoln. He learns to salute the flag, even though he can't understand the words. Too often Sunday schools also transmit these nationalistic emphases. In this case, Christianity is used to bless, to undergird what is

being done by the nation at the moment. This crisis, therefore, is not only the gimmicks to make things bigger and better but also the attempt to undergird, from a religious standpoint, national goals and policy. Evangelicals are especially tempted by this nationalistic folk religion.

6. The teaching ministry has not equipped persons to make decisions. For the most part persons sit and talk, sit and talk. Perhaps the bell at the end of the class allows persons to skirt issues and let decision-making to the pastor, to a committee, or to a conference organization. Increasingly, there is concern about the flow of decision-making in the churches. Churchwide boards and agencies have prepared statements and articulated positions on a host of issues—on peace, on race, on labor relations, on marriage, on recreation, to name a few. These come into existence through calling together a few expert and top officials for a study. Out of the study a findings committee prepares a report. This is, or becomes, the basis for a position statement. Then a churchwide board adopts it. Then comes the question, How can we get the people in the congregation to accept the statement, make it their own, and act on it? In the future, decisions will need to move in the opposite direction; the way must be found for decisions made in the local congregations to feed into a common consensus.

7. The teaching ministry does not stress action. Ross Bender spoke insightfully concerning this: [8]

The root does not lie in particular structures so that exchanging one set for another or getting rid of them altogether will not solve our problem. The root lies rather in our approach to teaching and learning. It lies in the fact that all too often we tend to assume that we know the will of God without doing it. . . . Picture a construction engineer and the foreman and workers who form his crew getting together once a week to consult their blueprints and drawings and discuss what a fine building they could build if they were building a building. Over a period of years they get together weekly and discuss it, but they never put up a building. Well, you see at once that the illustration is ridiculous because after a few weeks of this they'd all be fired and their firm would go bankrupt.

Or take my favorite illustration—imagine a football team in a huddle on the field. Let them develop a play—a good one with a kick or an end run. Then let them break up the huddle and scatter to their playing positions thinking about their good play while the other team is walking all over them.

Obviously, in each of these instances, the chain linking thought and discussion with decision-making and action is so essential that we cannot seriously entertain the thought of breaking it. The consequences are too disastrous. Only in the congregation do we tolerate the arm-chaired general mentality or the sidewalk superintendent mentality or the fan in the bleachers mentality whose chief distinction from the player on the field is that he only talks about the plays; he isn't on the ball. If he were down on the field, the whole matter would be rescued from the bleachers of abstraction and noninvolvement. With the ball in his hands and the opposing line of husky men in helmets and spikes converging on him, he would not merely content himself with considering the pros and cons of kicking, passing, or running. He would actually kick the ball or pass it or run with it for his life. . . .

8. Congregations have allowed the teaching ministry to become parallel rather than integral to their life and work. Already the Sunday school *and* church syndrome has been noted. But this is true also of women's work and of the way youth work has been structured. A lot of things go on in congregations, many times simultaneously, but do these programs converge on the mission of the church? Loyalties are built up to these organizations rather than to the congregation. Since this is discussed elsewhere, no more will be said here.

9. There is lack of clarity concerning the role of the minister in the teaching ministry. Because of the many, many teaching agencies within the congregation, the min-

ister scarcely knows where to fit in. As a result some ministers conclude that they should keep their hands off the whole teaching enterprise. The Sunday school, as an entity, is so well structured that the minister feels little need to become involved. All is in the hands of the superintendent. Further, since functioning in the educational structure is considered Christian service, no minister would want to displace a layman or hinder his opportunity to serve. Beneath this, and largely responsible for the confusion, is the inversion of the role of the layman and the role of the minister. It appears that to be a good layman one must become more and more like the minister. For example, on "Lay Sunday," to demonstrate what a good layman is able to do, he is asked to preach the sermon. The "good" layman functions when the congregation is gathered. He may lead in singing, be an ardent committee member, serve as a Sunday school teacher or superintendent. Apart from working hours, he is sealed off from his family and neighborhood as he gives evening after evening to work within the congregation. On the other hand, to be a good minister, he must become more and more like a layman. The minister is supposed to be out in the world witnessing. He is out telling people what the Bible teaches. He is out making evangelistic calls. He visits the sick. He prays at community functions. He tells who the Mennonites are. So the minister functions in the world and the layman functions in the congregation.

The New Testament suggests that the minister is called to function when the congregation is gathered. He is God's gift to the people of God. His task is to teach, to preach, to prepare members of the congregation for ministry in the world—for it is there that Christian service is Christian service—out among men. This notion underscores the need for the minister to be involved increasingly in the teaching ministry. In congregations, he is the only theologically trained person; his training must be made available to every member in the congregation.

10. Finally, and perhaps these are not facets of the crisis in the same sense as the others, two other observations should be made:

1. Little use of empirical research has been made in the teaching ministry. Christian educators have done little basic research. Little has been done to discover the relationships between theological belief and ethical behavior. Investigations that have been carried on have been largely programmatic research. This takes the form of field testing curriculum materials. It investigates backgrounds, opinions, and experiences of persons involved in the program. Research has been used to answer practical problems in the program rather than to discern more clearly the processes and results of Christian education. Christian educators, for the most part, have carried over results from educational research in developmental psychology, in the nature of personality, in group process, and teaching methods, even though the presuppositions, settings, and objectives of Christian education differ from general education.

2. It is important that churchwide boards and agencies which have educational aspects to their programs coordinate their efforts. Presently local congregations are the focal point for a wide range of programs, projects, and studies. As a result, congregations experience fieldmen coming to influence thinking, to encourage inauguration of programs in line with the emphasis of the sending board or agency. For example, at least four boards or agencies are encouraging congregations to make self-studies, but each from a different perspective—one emphasizes peace, another stewardship, another witness, another Christian education. Churchwide boards must look

at Christian education holistically, both in the congregation and across denominational structures. These fragmented approaches also illustrate the need for discerning what thinking should be done in congregations and what on the level of agencies and boards. The hope is that churchwide boards will work together closely, take a servant posture, and together assist congregations to be about their task in the world. The teaching ministry on all levels must reflect the unity of the nature and mission of the church.

So much for the crisis. This is not a call to scrap what is being done. Rather, this is a call to look again at areas needing exploration and change. The Spirit of God is present and working among the people of God. He will lead the church into ways that are relevant for this time.

Discussion Questions

1. What two dangers must we be aware of in the church, as suggested by Harold S. Bender? Discuss these in relation to your congregation.

2. Do you agree that there is a crisis in the teaching ministry of your congregation? To what degree are these symptoms in evidence in your congregation?

3. How much time is given each week to the teaching of the Christian faith in your congregation? Does this allow for good stewardship of buildings and equipment, considering the economic investment made in such facilities?

4. How can teaching and decision-making be brought together in the Sunday school class? Is the average Sunday school member capable of making decisions on religious issues?

5. How can we recover the New Testament views of the role of the minister and the role of the layman?

6. List some differences between the educational ministry of the church and that of the public school.

1. Harold S. Bender, *These Are My People*, p. 40.
2. *Ibid*, p. 65, 66.
3. See William Bean Kennedy, *The Shaping of Protestant Education*, for the story

of the coming of the Sunday school to North America and its role in the Protestant teaching ministry.

4. Harold S. Bender, *Mennonite Sunday School Centennial, 1840-1940.*

5. "Letter" in Archives, Mennonite Historical Library, Goshen, Ind.

6. One congregation built a $200,000 building for the one-hour-per-week, simultaneous teaching program and ended up employing a full-time janitor to keep the building clean.

7. Rolfe Lanier Hunt notes these tensions:

Public School Education Says:	*Christian Education Says:*
a. Obey the state	a. Obeying God is higher duty
b. Value intellect and knowledge	b. Value the heart, right with God
c. Keep the body strong and healthy, take the animal satisfactions	c. My body is God's gift to be used as He wills
d. Be a patriot	d. Be a world citizen
e. The well-being of society is important	e. God loves each individual
f. Belong	f. Be a prophet, a pioneer

8. Address at Mennonite General Conference, 1965.

4

The Context for Christian Education

So far, the centrality of teaching among God's people across the centuries, the development of the present strategy, and something of the crisis facing the teaching ministry in the congregation during the latter third of the twentieth century have been explored.

For some, these pages are likely too critical or overly judgmental. They might ask, "Is there anything good in what we are doing?" Clearly, there is much good in our present program, and there are many indications of sound achievement in the past. The fact that time is taken to reevaluate is itself an expression of confidence and of hope that what is good might become better. Our purpose is reconstruction, to point in other directions which, hopefully, may contribute to a more viable teaching ministry.

The Congregation, the Context

The context for the teaching ministry is the local congregation. The congregation is the fellowship of those who have found Jesus as Lord and Savior and who are following Him in obedience. When viewed in this way, the congregation includes the home where Christian teaching takes place, both formally and informally. If the teaching ministry is to be meaningful, it must reflect and be involved in the total life of the congregation. It must move the congregation toward God's purpose for it.

In Romans 9, Paul describes the mystery of God's working, calling both Jews and Gentiles into His family. Paul quotes the prophet Hosea (verses 25, 26):

> Those who were not my people
> I will call "my people,"
> and her who was not beloved
> I will call "my beloved."
>
> And in the very place where it was
> said to them, "You are not my
> people,"
> they will be called "sons of the
> living God."

The theme of this passage is the *becoming* of a people who were not. Richard C. Detweiler sees the congregation as "the becoming of a people in response to the gospel in a specific time and place." [1] This agrees with 1 Peter 2: 9, 10. The church is also referred to as an *assembly*, the community of believers in Christ called *out of* the world. Yet this community of believers in Christ is called together *in* the world, and is called together *for* the world.

A People Who Were Not

Returning to Romans, Paul wrote, "In the very place where it was said to them, 'You are not my people,' they will be called 'sons of the living God.' " Here it is clear that a congregation is the coming together of a people *who were not the people* of God. This is hard to grasp and to keep in the forefront. Yet, this is at the heart of the understanding of the nature of the church within the believer's church tradition. The realization of being a people who were not a people (1 Peter 2:10) is easily lost. Perhaps this is due to the current emphasis on Christian education in its derived form which spends so much time with children. As products of this approach, persons feel that the congregation has always been, when a sense of not having been is needed. Educational programs point to historical origins, to 1525, to migrations to North America, emphasizing continuity. A shift of view is needed, to see that the church is not an institution set up for joining; rather, it is a people being called forth. These people, responding to the gospel and in the process of becoming the people of God, form the congregation. Neither traditional virtues nor ethnic connections form the base—it is relationship, relationship to God, to their brethren in Christ, and to persons who have not yet responded in faith to what God has done in Christ.

Relationships

This view of the congregation has profound implications for the teaching ministry. For one thing, it becomes clear that the teaching ministry hangs more on interpersonal relationships than upon institutional forms. Human beings do need institutions and structures. This is part of the human predicament. However, among a people who are becoming, personal relationships will be expressed through the forms, as opposed to fitting persons into forms and structures and attempting to create relationships therein. In other words, this view of congregations begins with people with a mission and with relationships channeled through forms, rather than beginning with forms and structures and attempting to fit people into them. The present strategy involves the perpetuation of teaching agencies. To keep the agencies going, we force persons into these structures instead of allowing the structures to grow out of the gifts of persons, their sense of call, the needs of the situation, and the congregation's sense of purpose.

God is calling congregations, in more ways than we recognize, to be a new people. Fortunately, Mennonites are losing their identity as a rural and an ethnic people. New insights are emerging concerning past tendencies to confuse cultural practices with the Christian life. Fewer persons are ready to say that to lose distinctive attire or to lose the German language is to lose the essence of Mennonitism. To see the congregation as a people "who were not a people" in the process of becoming, is to see the church coming into being in communities with centuries of Mennonite history as well as in the inner city or on other continents. It is impressive to see new and creative fellowships being brought into being among high rises of St. Louis, or in the heart of Chicago or New York City. Mennonite World Conference impresses this further, as brethren assemble from many races, nationalities, cultural backgrounds, and economic levels.

Becoming at a Specific Time and Place

Paul also suggests (Romans 9:26) that the congregation is the becoming of a people at a specific time and place. "And in the very place where it was said to them, 'You are not my people,' they will be called 'sons of the living God.' " Since the congregation is on earth, the people are human; they have problems; they are sinful; they have needs; they are connected with the power structures in the world. To avoid the reality of this, there has been a tendency to promote a high view of the church, of what it ought to be, but a low view of the congregation, because here it is easy to see things as they really are.

Of course, it is enjoyable to go back to the Anabaptists and to claim they provided a model for the church today— pure and simple, loving and obedient, evangelistic, etc. However, if a congregation is the becoming of a people in a specific time and place, and this is taken seriously, the task is not to develop an abstract view of what the church ought to be while everything goes on as usual. Rather, the task is to see the congregation as it really is—weak, sinful, limited, and in need of God's grace and forgiveness; in repentance, confess sin, failure, tensions, and receive God's grace and power to become the people of God in this time and place. The people of God are formed as they respond to God in repentance and faith, to what He has done in Jesus Christ, and allow the Holy Spirit to work in and through them in the world. Becoming in a specific time and place requires that those engaged in the teaching ministry, for example, hear and answer the Word of God instead of continuing without question the many, many good teaching agencies that have been borrowed or have come upon us. This is flexibility in its best sense.

Flexibility and Involvement

Since a congregation is not static, its teaching ministry dare not be static. Harold S. Bender was helpful at this point. He wrote, "A congregation is a people, believing, worshiping, obeying, and witnessing." If a congregation is seen as a thriving, moving, pulsating body, then it is hard to define a model for the teaching ministry. It is possible to say, "This is how it was," without casting judgment on the sincerity and integrity of those persons who brought current structures into being. It is possible to say, "This is how it is now." This places responsibility upon the congregation to look, to listen, and to respond obediently to whatever God is calling. To say, "This is how it will be in the future," will depend upon present obedience. At the root of the current crisis is failure to be alert and ready to respond to what God is calling the church to do and be in the world at this moment. God is acting (we all believe that), and we must act. Discernment and obedience are necessary. Seeing what God is doing is discernment. Doing what He calls us to do is obedience. These can not be divided, for where there is no obedience, there is no more discernment.

Abraham provides an important illustration for those in the teaching ministry. He went out not knowing where he was going, but he was going in obedience. He was not like those who say, "Let's not change until we're sure the new is better than the old," or who are constantly looking back to what was.

Concepts of flexibility and involvement in the world are difficult for many to comprehend. Ways of doing things have become sacred. Further, they have been taught that the church and the world are separate; that Christ is in the church and the devil is in the world. The Christian's task, they have been told, is to keep the church pure. This is done by building walls of separation while sending out, of course, a few strong members to witness in the world, to bring "souls" back to the safety of the church. With this posture they were concerned with saving themselves in the midst of the world rather than with becoming God's people, involved in the world, reconciling men with God and with men.

The Life Together

The congregation as the context for Christian education suggests this hypothesis: the more the congregation approximates God's intention for it, the more effective its teaching ministry will be. The New Testament goes to great length to describe the quality of life in the congregation. In the congregation, redeemed men are members one of another. Romans 12:5. There is love one for another. John 13:34, 35; Galatians 5:13; 1 Thessalonians 3:12. There is the same mind one toward another. Romans 12:16. One edifies another. Romans 14:19. There is admonition. Romans 15:14. There is care one for another. 1 Corinthians 12:25. There is service one for another. Galatians 5:13. There is bearing of one another's burdens. Galatians 6:2. There is forbearance of one another. Ephesians 5:21. There is comforting one another. 1 Thessalonians 4:18. There is confessing of faults one to another. James 5:16. There is prayer one for another. James 5:16. There is fellowship one with another. 1 John 1 7. There is hospitality one to another. 1 Peter 4:9.

Here learning can take place because life and relationships of faith are demonstrated. Neither a program nor a curriculum can be effective in a congregation that is torn with conflict or at the point of division. All that should be taught about reconciliation, about the end of hostility at the cross, and about love and concern for brethren and for the world is lost in the midst of battle. With this climate no wonder the church can scarcely respond to the agenda the world brings to it, let alone be a force for Christ in the world. Who in the church or in the world will take seriously the claims of the church for the gospel if its own life does not authenticate its words? Perhaps the inability of the church to be a force in the world can be traced to congregations and their failure to be communities of love, in which the full implications of the gospel are demonstrated by word and deed.

The congregation, as the context for the teaching ministry, suggests that the teaching ministry must be related to the entire life and work of the congregation. It is not merely what happens in Sunday school or in another teaching agency. As noted above, for too long Christian education has been seen as tied to teaching agencies rather than a ministry that undergirds all that the congregation does in transmitting the faith, in preparing people for service, in helping people worship, and in discerning God's will. Wherever education is needed to communicate all that Jesus taught, to equip the saints for witness in the world, in short, to assist the people of God in becoming, there the teaching ministry must function.

Each person in the congregation is affected by and has an effect upon the teaching ministry. As persons are responsive to God's call, they create a climate in which other persons become aware of God's self-disclosure. Associating with others in the community of faith permits one to receive from and contribute to the faith of others. Each brings and each receives and together responding to the Word, to the Spirit, and to each other, the congregation becomes. This underscores again the importance of flexibility.

The view of the congregation as the people of God becoming is not characterized by an intense concern to get rid of organizations and agencies in order to find something new, nor is it characterized by tenaciously clinging to forms whose usefulness is past. This view does not define congregation in any primary sense in terms of structure and forms, or organizations and programs; rather, it is defined in terms of a living response to the living, present, acting God. Because the primary focus or orientation is not upon its forms and structures, the faithful congregation can be relaxed and flexible as it makes whatever modifications and adaptations are necessary in its teaching ministry to be a discerning and obedient community carrying on Christ's work in the world.

Discussion Questions

1. What is meant by "becoming the people of God"?

2. How do proper interpersonal relationships and institutional forms contribute to the church's fulfilling its ministry?

3. What attitude should the congregation take toward forms and structures in its teaching efforts?

4. Should the teaching ministry focus on preparing persons to be "in the world" or to be "not of the world"?

5. Why is the informal teaching of the congregation as important as the formal teaching?

1. Richard C. Detweiler, "What Is a Congregation?" Address at Mennonite General Conference, 1965.

5

The Objective for Christian Education

We have viewed the congregation as a people who were no people, but who are becoming a people at a specific time and place in response to God's activity. Such a congregation has a teaching ministry in obedience to Jesus Christ. The ministry, however, is characterized by flexibility as it equips persons to participate in the mission of the church. This view requires that purposes of the teaching ministry coincide with those of the church. Two objectives are not possible, as though there were an objective for the church and another for the teaching ministry. Indeed, care must be exercised lest what is done in the teaching ministry through a variety of agencies or settings is not at variance with the primary commitment of the church.

Over the years Christian educators have sensed the need for the place of objectives. In the 1800's their objective was simply to teach a knowledge of the Bible. Pupils listened to Bible stories. They memorized Bible verses. It was assumed that growth in Christian character would follow, somehow, automatically. In the early 1900's objectives were broadened to include concerns for personal and social living. Life situations were emphasized. But this was not without opposition. In the Mennonite Church "graded"

Sunday school lessons were not released until 1959, twenty years later than they should have been, because certain leaders thought "graded" lessons meant dealing with life situations rather than Bible content. The *Gospel Herald*, before 1940, contained frequent articles against graded Sunday school lessons, many of them written by the editor, whose opposition carried much weight.

The Twelve Objectives

When work began on graded Sunday school lessons in 1952, planners had to raise the question of objectives. What are we trying to accomplish? During 1953 groups struggled with this question. The result was the publication of a booklet, *Objectives for Christian Education Curriculum Materials*, in 1955. This stated objectives in twelve areas, [1] in terms of outcomes in the lives of persons from primary through young people. This work helped planners see the broad scope of Christian education and the wide range of outcomes that might be anticipated through the educational process.

Each of the twelve areas was subdivided into six to twelve outcomes which were also spelled out on the primary, junior, intermediate, senior, and young people's levels. Though objectives were couched in behavioral outcomes, or so it was thought, they were not of the measurable kind—"to understand," "to appreciate," "to grasp." Some, however, were measurable, such as "to memorize," or "to use." These objectives provided something of a mosaic for developing curriculum materials. They were not focused on a dynamic mission of the church. Thus they did not contribute a clear sense of direction. In reality, the objectives were intermediate ones. They were stated in the context of an implicit rather than explicit overall strategy or objective. The objectives were like many streams but without a source or ultimate destiny clearly indicated. The twelve categories were important ones, and a good job was done discerning some possible outcomes at various points along the life-span.

Likely, this effort would not be duplicated today. Campbell Wyckoff put his finger on the difficulty with this approach which was characteristic of that time:

Most often the objectives of Christian education have been stated in terms of the great concerns of the Christian faith and the Christian life. Such objectives, for all that they prefix such phrases as "to help pupils know," or "to develop in growing persons," actually constitute analyses of curriculum content or scope. Sometimes useful as statements of scope, such statements fail at two points: (1) They are too detailed to focus the objective of Christian education sharply. (2) They are often too brief to do justice to the range of relationships involved in a way that is really helpful for direction in curriculum building. [2]

The twelve areas, compounded by sub-points, multiplied by departmental levels, made the objectives almost impossible to comprehend, let alone synthesize and give direction to the curriculum project. Furthermore, statements of anticipated behavioral outcomes are increasingly suspected among Christian educators today because of the obvious tendency toward behavioristic psychology they portray. Now we are concerned that persons be free to respond to God's revelation with behavior evoked by the Spirit. We do not want to manipulate persons or to condition them to predetermined forms of behavior. Today there is reaction to the 1955 objectives because of the implicit moralism reflected in them. Finally, the objectives were far from complete. In addition to objectives found in the book, there are teacher's objectives, group objectives, and a wide range of objectives that are embedded in the gospel and focused by various biblical and theological themes that were untouched.

One Objective

In addition to the shortcomings noted above, other factors were at work, helping us see the need for another kind of objective that would allow for greater freedom and flexibility, yet provide the necessary focus. [3] Among these factors were:

1. We began to see that Christian education must undergird the entire work of the church, equipping persons to participate in the mission of the church.

2. We came to see that Christian education must assume that the gospel is relevant to all of man's life and to all of his relationships. We knew this when we worked on objectives in the last decade, but as time went on, the impression deepened.

3. We began to see that Christian education must reflect the God-given unity of the nature and the mission of the church. We saw the need to eliminate the divisiveness that crept into the teaching ministry as the work of the church was divided to make it manageable without provision for coordination of the work. Somehow, it had to be made clear to all concerned that the church has one mission and that all ministries must contribute to that mission.

4. We began to see Christian education as a mutual learning experience, in which persons tested one another, corrected one another, and enlarged one another's understanding, while wrestling with the issues of life in the light of revelation. Christian education was not merely transmitting to the "grass roots" insights or decisions of the elite.

5. We noted the changing view of the relation between church and world. In years past, teaching emphasized that Christians were not *of* the world. Now we began to see the other side of the equation—that Christians were also *in* the world. We saw that many Christians were poorly

equipped to be *in* the world and at the same time not *of* the world.

6. We became aware of the need for education across the life-span and especially for adult education. The energies of the church had gone almost exclusively to childhood education. We, like others, were caught up with child development or with child evangelism. It is not clear how much was bought from either side, except to note that this emphasis was somehow detached from our primary commitment to a believer's church with a responsible adult membership. Because of this emphasis upon teaching children, the church did not provide significant education for adults which dealt with making homes Christian, with occupational issues, with standards of living, with use of leisure time, with stewardship, with civic responsibility, with witnessing, with developing Christian interpersonal relationships, with retirement, with old age, with loneliness, or with sickness and death.

7. We saw, as noted earlier, the need for greater flexibility in the teaching ministry which suggested moving away from teaching agencies with fixed variables.

8. We saw the need for churchwide boards and committees to perceive more clearly what the teaching ministry is all about, and to focus their work on helping the congregation fulfill its mission.

The Objective

These notions demanded a new look at the question of objectives. In 1963, Christian educators, representatives of churchwide boards, pastors, and theologians from several Mennonite groups wrestled with this question. The outcome of this study was a single objective:

Through Christian education, the church seeks to help all persons to know God as revealed supremely in Jesus Christ and the Scriptures; to become aware of who they are, of what their situation is, and of their alienation to the end that they may repent of their sin, respond to God's redeeming love in faith, and become members of the body of Christ; to grow in Christ within the community of believers; to walk in the Spirit in every relationship; to fulfill the call to discipleship in the world; and to abide in the Christian hope.

Reasons for an Objective

In working with this objective, it became more clear why an objective is necessary for Christian education:

1. It helps to determine the direction of the process, what the ultimate purpose is.

2. It provides a standard for developing and evaluating short-term goals.

3. It helps to determine the methods and procedures that will be used in the process.

4. It provides a basis for selectivity and organizing resources.

5. It provides a way to measure progress and achievement.

6. It provides a basis for evaluation of both process and product.

7. It ensures relevance.

8. It helps to bring unity to the enterprise. [4]

Characteristics of an Objective

Ross Bender has noted the following characteristics of a good objective:

1. It should be clear and simple.
2. It should be foundational.
3. It should be comprehensive.
4. It should be realistic, that is, attainable.
5. It should provide guidance for the enterprise.
6. It should be measurable.

7. It should be true to the gospel.

8. It should be in harmony with and undergird the purpose of the church.

9. It should be relevant to contemporary life situations of persons.

10. It should be flexible enough to allow participation by those being educated in the formulation of sub-goals derived from it; in other words, it should guarantee that the freedom and integrity of persons are not violated.

11. It must be appropriate to every person, whatever his age across the life-span, whatever stage of development or maturity.

12. It should comprehend both content and experience in the proper interrelationship and not set them at variance with each other.

13. It should allow for shifting priorities as needs and circumstances change. [5]

Exegeting the Objective

To develop an objective with the characteristics listed above is a large order, and yet the objective measures up quite well. To work with this objective, it is important to understand what it means.

1. This objective is long-term. That is, it can be achieved and yet it cannot be achieved. It is not as though one could achieve it and then ask, "What next?" The nature of the objective is that it requires growth and continued growth toward its achievement. It assumes "becoming."

2. This objective speaks to "all persons" across the life-span. It has relevance for persons from preschool to old age. For example, this objective provided guidance in developing curriculum for four- and five-year-old children. It is addressed to the fundamental questions young chil-

dren ask: Who am I? Why am I here? Who is God?

3. This objective is rooted in the gospel and focuses on the mission of the church. There is concern that all persons come "to know God as revealed supremely in Jesus Christ and the Scriptures." The emphasis upon Scripture is significant. The objective in a real sense begins with revelation. It provides the posture for the preschool curriculum mentioned above. In general, children's workers have been reluctant to begin with the nature of man, the Word of God, and the biblical theology. They have been concerned primarily with the developmental tasks of children in growing toward "the Christian way of life," and secondarily with the child's need for coming to know God's word to him, God's plan for him, and the supreme end of human life to live in fellowship with God, here and hereafter. This objective shifts the focus. Curriculum planners ask first, What is God doing and saying which enables humans to know themselves and to know God? How can this Word of God, these actions of God, become meaningful and their relevance understood at every level of maturity?

4. This objective is general. It does not list specific beliefs, yet it deals with the fundamental questions concerning God, self, personal relationships, and purpose of life.

5. This objective is evangelistic. It is concerned that "all persons" come to know God.

6. This objective declares that the congregation, "the community of believers," is the context for Christian education.

7. This objective embraces both Christian experience and Christian discipleship. On one hand it speaks of walking in the Spirit; on the other, of living as a disciple in the world. Thus, the personal and social aspects of the gospel are emphasized. This objective assumes that there is nothing outside of the concern of the gospel of Christ.

8. This objective is concerned with hope, for life here as well as life hereafter.

9. This objective is something of a cycle: a person comes to know God, he becomes aware of himself, he responds to God in repentance and faith, he becomes a part of the church, he grows in Christ in discipleship and in the Christian hope, he enters the world to help all persons to know God, to become aware of who they are, etc.

This objective has set in motion forces that are changing our approach to Christian education. It forces us to rethink both the role and the nature of the congregation. It takes us from questions dealing with the mechanics of running a Sunday school to the fundamental issues undergirding the teaching ministry, such as questions about our reason for existence.

As the objective is exegeted, certain phrases or clauses stand out:

1. *To help*. The church seeks "to help." This is an important posture. This is over against seeking to legislate, or to tell, or to command.

2. *To know God*. This is central. Knowing involves relationship, an interaction of personalities. It comes by way of Jesus, the Scriptures, the Holy Spirit, and the brotherhood.

3. *To become aware*. This is to have revealed something of one's self, of what one is, and of what one's need is.

Then there are the words that describe the continuing experience of a people who were no people, becoming the people of God: *repent, respond, become, grow, walk*. These words suggest a turning to God in faith, becoming a part of Christ's body, growing like Him among the believers, and walking as He walked. These words recognize the unpredictability of the work of the Spirit in the teaching ministry. We are less sure of our ability to predict or to project outcomes. From one standpoint, the 1955 book of objectives may reflect arrogance rather than dependence upon the Spirit, allowing Him to call forth His own responses in His own way.

1. To fulfill. This is to demonstrate in the world the life of Jesus Christ.

2. To abide. Here is confidence for this life and for the life to come.

An objective has been stated. No one is coerced to accept it. It does reflect much thought, striving, and attempting to see something of the nature of the congregation, its mission in the world, and the place of teaching in the congregation. To begin with, this objective pinpoints what is being attempted. We have found that it opens doors to many new insights that are not possible through the traditional approaches to Christian education, which promote the present structures, trying to make them bigger and better.

Discussion Questions

1. Why are objectives needed in Christian education? Why have understandings concerning objectives changed?

2. What guidance does the objective on page seventy-nine give to the teaching ministry in your congregation?

3. What is meant by a "long-term" objective?

4. In determining the objective for Christian education, do you begin with man or with God's revelation?

1. I. Bible Knowledge and Use
    II. Salvation
    III. Christian Beliefs About God
    IV. Discipleship
    V. Church Fellowship
    VI. Worship
    VII. Witnessing
    VIII. Stewardship
    IX. The Christian Home
    X. Christian Social Relations
    XI. Nonconformity
    XII. Christian Citizenship

2. Campbell Wyckoff, *Theory and Design of Christian Education Curriculum,* p. 63.

3. For a helpful discussion of objective see *The Church's Educational Ministry: A Curriculum Plan,* pp. 8-11.

4. Adapted from *The Objective for Christian Education: An Interpretation,* Ross Bender, June 14, 1965.

5. *Ibid.*

6

Settings for Christian Education

What is a setting? Those raised on a farm might think of a hen sitting on a lot of eggs. This isn't it, even though Christian educators have laid a lot of eggs! "Setting" is the name given to "a particular structure which is planned and organized to provide teaching-learning opportunities within the total educational ministry. [1] The use of a word like "setting" may keep the congregation from thinking solely in terms of teaching agencies like Sunday school or summer Bible school. Teaching agencies are settings too, but in them the variables have become frozen or fixed. In thinking about settings, at least ten variables have been identified. [2] By experimenting with these variables, it may be possible for congregations to develop more relevant and more effective forms for the teaching ministry as the congregation is in the process of becoming the people of God.

The Variables

1. The distinctive contribution. What is unique about this setting? What distinctive contribution does this setting make to the total teaching ministry that no other one can do as well? In other words, What can be done more effectively here than at any other time or place? This is a

simple question, but it has seldom been asked. Suppose, for example, that we have the distinctive contribution of a Sunday school class well in mind. Why is it when the congregation moves to a camp setting the Sunday school class is duplicated as part of the camp program? Camp ends up as Sunday school under the trees! This variable makes congregations ask not only, What is the unique contribution of the Sunday school class? but also, What is the unique contribution of camping? This variable forces the congregation to explore the distinct contribution of each part of the program. This variable keeps the congregation from doing the same thing in each of its settings, as it emphasizes that which is distinctive or unique.

2. The duration. In other words, is this setting available continuously throughout the year, year after year? Is it available only in the summer? Or for a weekend? Years ago, when Sunday school was not held year-round, "evergreen" Sunday schools were promoted. The duration of Sunday school was extended throughout the entire year through "evergreen" promotion.

3. Frequency. This variable refers to the number of meetings. Is it annual? Monthly? Weekly? Or is it a one-shot meeting?

4. Time span. This refers to the amount of time required for effective work in the setting. Is it one hour? Is it two hours? Is it a nine-hour session? Is it twenty-four hours, as in a retreat?

5. Location. This variable refers to the place of the meeting. Does it meet in the church building? Under the trees? In a building downtown? In a home?

6. Constituency. This variable asks, Who is involved? Families? Children? Teenagers? Young married adults? Unmarried adults?

7. Grouping. This variable asks how persons are

grouped. In one large group? In small groups? According to age? By families? Grouped around common interests?

8. Administrative connection. This variable refers to the way the setting is tied in to the overall strategy for the teaching ministry. It asks, Who is responsible? How are the responsible persons appointed? To whom do they report?

9. Resources. What is needed for teaching-learning in this structure? Printed materials? Books? Projected materials? What budget is needed?

10. Leadership. Who is responsible to help the group move toward the accomplishment of the distinctive contribution?

A setting derives its form from the interplay of these ten variables. Again it should be noted that a teaching agency is a construct in which variables have become rigid or have become fixed. Thus Sunday school has fixed variables from congregation to congregation. It is year-round; it meets once a week; it lasts an hour; it is held in the church building; it is for everyone; it is grouped according to age; the superintendent provides the administrative connection; printed curriculum pieces are needed.

Experimenting with these ten variables, however, opens up a host of new ways for using Sunday morning settings. For example, if "distinctive contribution" were perceived differently, this could lead to lengthening sessions from one hour to two hours. As the Hindu suggested, "You should have class every other Sunday and then have two hours for discussion."

Some Presuppositions

An emphasis upon "settings" rather than upon "agencies" involves certain presuppositions. For one thing, it presupposes that the congregation is the focal point and context for the teaching ministry, and not a teaching agency no matter how old or how firmly fixed its variables.

Settings presuppose that the congregation functions both as a gathered and as a scattered community. These settings may be located in the meetinghouse, in homes, or in unexpected places in the world. The objective helps the congregation experiment with these variables, since it too is concerned with witnessing for a verdict. Thus the person who becomes a Christian is to perform the mission of the church, to walk in the Spirit in every relationship, to fulfill the call of discipleship in the world, and to abide in a Christian hope. This involves all members—serving and witnessing wherever they are. The person is taught for the gathered life—doctrine, history, morality; and for the scattered life—apostleship, discipleship, stewardship. The gathered life and the scattered life open many new settings for Christian education that would not be possible if the congregation focused only on the gathered life. David Hunter says that the scattered life of the church suggests a whole new range of settings:

If the scattered church trains the laity for their ministries in the scattered world of secular institutions, it would seem logical that the gathering itself be at the places which are appropriate for training the laity for their scattered life. [3]

Revitalizing or Redirecting Familiar Settings

Instead of trying to create or to discover completely new settings, it might be better to try to revitalize, redirect, or unfreeze the variables of our present teaching agencies to see what might be done as variables are arranged or related in different ways. For example, daily vacation Bible school is a teaching agency. It has the duration of two weeks in the summer. Its frequency is once a year.

Its time span is two hours. It is located in the church building. The constituency are children of the congregation and community. Suppose the constituency variable were changed to include adults, and thus a new form of adult education. Now suppose further that the congregation would employ a professional teacher to provide a two-week course on college level, and for college credit as part of the congregation's intraining or ongoing educational ministry. Note that changing this variable would indicate change in another—the distinctive contribution. What would happen if each teaching agency were examined to see wherein variables might be changed to focus on preparing persons to witness and to serve?

Perhaps it would be helpful to list some of the settings in the congregation that are available to the teaching ministry: Sunday morning, Sunday evening, midweek meetings, meetings in homes, youth fellowship, children's meetings, business meetings, men's fellowships, women's meetings, clubs, membership classes, vacation Bible school, Bible conferences, revival meetings, family events, leadership training, outreach opportunities, committees, and board meetings. A whole raft of things are going on now.

Beyond the congregation are camps, conference retreats, family settings, public and private schools (with shared and released time), settings for service—voluntary service and Pax, witness workshops, conventions, and ecumenical study courses. In many of these, the variables are quite fixed.

Imagine a congregation aware of itself as a people in the process of becoming, having its objective for the teaching ministry clearly in view, but wanting to revitalize and redirect its program rather than to create new settings. What might it do? For one thing the congregation might try to *increase integration between truth and action* within its present structures. Or, it might provide for *more personal interaction*, for more face-to-face encounter on depth levels. Or, it might provide opportunities for *personal involvement* in social work, in service activities, and in evangelistic witnessing, thus relating the congregation to the community. Or, it might consider how to provide more effectively for the *needs of each person* within the congregation, for each child, for each adult, for the single as well as the married, for each person with exceptional needs. (The church has done a poor job providing for exceptional persons—whether advanced intellectually, retarded intellectually, or handicapped physically. Too little also has been done for the unmarried women.) Or, it might provide for *interaction with Christians beyond the congregation.* Any one of these could revitalize teaching-learning in current structures.

Providing for Personal Interaction

Suppose a congregation wants to experiment with the Sunday morning hour in order to provide for more personal interaction. What might it do? It could experiment with the grouping variable.

1. It might set up a group to discuss the morning sermon, to come to grips with what was said. (Incidentally, not many groups are able to deal with two major issues in two consecutive hours as is required in Sunday school *and* church.)

2. It might set up new groups. How many congregations have given much thought as to how adults are grouped on Sunday morning? For the most part, adults are treated just like children. Because educators believe that pre-schoolers should be together, that intermediates should be together, and that young people should be together, Sunday school leaders have also decided that adults should

be divided on the basis of age. So adults 20 to 35 years of age are together, adults 35 to 50 are together, adults 50 to 75 are together, and those beyond 75 are together. Thus, for the average adult the notable progress in his educational experience is movement from one class to another as he grows older. To provide personal interaction, is it best to group by age?

3. Why not group adults alphabetically? See what kind of mix that makes. This could be quite interesting as persons from young to old are together and there would be interaction across generations.

4. Why not group adults geographically? Were adults grouped geographically, those living in a given area would see more clearly their responsibilities to be servants and witnesses there. They could invite a neighbor to church. The neighbor would participate in the area study group instead of being shunted off to a class of strangers of the same age. Geographic organization would put the neighbor with the people he came to church with. Geographic grouping would encourage persons to think about, pray for, and serve in the area they live. It would provide opportunities to help those in the community experience difficulty or hardships. Geographic grouping would be a base for movement back into the community as witnesses and servants.

5. Why not group adults on the basis of their interests? Flexibility of program suggests that a wide range of course offerings will be necessary. More will be needed than the Uniform Series provides. Adults should be counseled concerning what they would prefer to study. With a range of course offerings, adults could be grouped according to interest. Interest also contributes to greater personal interaction.

6. Why not group adults according to ability? It might

be good to get those together who do not or will not study or prepare for class sessions. Put them in an elementary class! Those who want to study—put together. Those who want to stay on the surface put in another group. Why should those who want to study on a deeper level be held back by the disinterested and the incompetent? Standardized Bible knowledge tests might provide a basis or device for determining who should be in which group. Put those with high Bible knowledge in one group and those with little in another.

These have been a few suggestions for experimenting with one variable, grouping, in order to secure greater personal interaction. The possibilities of experimentation with other variables to revitalize the teaching ministry seem almost endless. Experimenting with "time span," experimenting with "resources," or experimenting with "location" offers other exciting possibilities.

Too few adults have opportunities to interact with Christians from other denominations or with members of the same denomination from neighboring congregations. Homes could provide the settings for assembling new constituencies. Women invite neighbors to coffee and turn discussions to spiritual matters. Factories and business establishments also provide opportunities for prayer and study fellowships of Christians from many backgrounds. Recently a manager of a large store in the downtown area of one of our major cities told me about a group of managers who get together periodically to pray, to study the Bible, and to help one another make ethical decisions in the business world.

Suppose the congregation became concerned about personal involvement. It might be helpful for the congregation to become aware of the many organizations in which members are already participating. An inventory should be taken of the organizations, the clubs, the civic groups, and the service groups which are (or should be) witnessed to by the presence of congregation members. Such an inventory would help the congregation sense that each church member is part of its strategy for winning the world for Christ as he functions in each organization.

In addition, the congregation should become aware of the many occupations of its members. Years ago, most members would have been farmers, but this is hardly the case today. Now there are factory workers, businessmen, tradesmen. Women are in the professional and nonprofessional jobs. There are the retired and professional men of all kinds—lawyers, doctors, teachers, and professors. Clearly, members of the congregation are functioning in most of the arenas of the world. The question no longer is how to take the church to the world. The fact is, the church is in the world. The task of the teaching ministry, as stated earlier, is to prepare each Christian to live as a witness and servant in the world. Each Christian in his profession or occupation is to function as an extension of the congregation.

In this view, the congregation, therefore, is not only the context for preparing persons; it is also the base of support for the Christian's witness and service in the world. In the congregation he is taught and receives counsel. Wherever he goes, he is undergirded by the prayer and concern of his brethren. The many needs, the many opportunities, the focus on becoming, underscore anew the need for flexibility for discerning new ways to interrelate variables, so that the congregation may indeed equip persons for service and witness when gathered, and support and pray for one another when scattered.

Administration

Finally, a word should be said about administration for a flexible program. Flexibility suggests that a single administrative structure is not valid everywhere. If each congregation is in the process of becoming in its situation, it must build its own program. The "universal" models of Sunday school and vacation Bible school may be replaced by new forms as congregations take their situation, their gifts, and their mission seriously. When congregations had a full house of teaching agencies, work was coordinated by representatives from the Sunday school, summer Bible school, Sunday evening service, boys' and girls' clubs, women's organizations, etc., forming a board of education. Whatever wholeness was achieved was by way of such integration. Increasingly, such integrating boards are sensing their helplessness as representatives approach problems from the standpoint of agencies with fixed variables. In these coordinating groups the possibility of change is difficult to perceive—maintenance, perpetuation, scheduling, and working at jurisdictional disputes become the main agenda items.

However, in congregations attempting flexibility, another form of administration is emerging—which keeps the congregation central, which recognizes gifts, and which looks at the teaching ministry whole, across the life-span instead of piecemeal, agency by agency, or department by department.

An emerging structure which by its simplicity could enjoy widespread application has three foci: (1) curriculum, (2) personnel, and (3) home and church relationships. These foci find expression in three groups which do not emphasize agencies as such. Rather, they are aware of all the settings available in the congregation's teaching ministry. The curriculum group studies *what* is being done in each setting. It looks for comprehensiveness and balance in what is taught across the life-span. At the head of the curriculum group is the pastor. Through this, the long-sought integration between teaching and preaching has the possibility of achievement. This also tends to make the minister's theological training available to the congregation. This allows the minister to make significant strides in recovering his teaching ministry. In short, the curriculum group sees whole what is being preached and what is being taught in the congregation. It recommends to trustees needed facilities and equipment.

The teaching ministry needs people whether the agency or any other approach is used. A personnel group works alongside the curriculum group calling and preparing persons to serve in the teaching ministry. The personnel group is aware of personnel needs for all settings of the congregation. It is also aware of the gifts and abilities in the congregation and of those with a sense of call. The personnel group, keeping the total teaching ministry in view, eliminates the competition for teachers and other workers which occurs as teaching agencies search for staff persons. No longer does each agency ask, "Who will be *our* teachers this year?" and then proceed to recruit with the result that a good teacher may be approached by a half-dozen agencies requesting his service. The personnel group is also responsible for training leaders and teachers for service in the various settings.

The home and church group looks at interrelationships between teaching in the congregation and teaching in the home. It sees the family as part of the context for Christian education. This group attempts to sense needs among parents, among older people, among children and youth, and feeds these concerns into planning for the total educational ministry. The group precipitates meetings of parents of teenagers, for example, to discuss problems and relationships. It makes sure that the teaching ministry of the congregation supports the home in its task. Three groups like these are possible in very small congregations. These work together to plan the overall teaching and preaching for the congregation. The administrative pattern integrates the teaching ministry in a way that is almost impossible under current agency patterns which have built-in competition, jurisdictional disputes, poor scheduling, fragmentation of effort, and the uncoordinated use in personnel. Financing for the teaching ministry would be carried on through regular congregational channels. There is no need for a multiplicity of treasurers as found frequently in the agency approach.

Seeing the distinct contributions of settings whether new or old, experimenting with the variables, looking at the teaching ministry whole, preparing persons across the life-span for participation in the mission of the church, this is the exciting task before those engaged in the congregation's teaching ministry.

Discussion Questions

1. What is meant by a "setting"?

2. In a given setting can you think of variables in addition to the ten listed?

3. Make a list of settings which are available to your congregation in addition to those already in use.

4. How can flexibility be built into new teaching settings so that the variables will not become fixed, thus giving rise to more "teaching agencies"?

5. Examine your Sunday evening service to see wherein fixed variables might be changed in order to prepare persons to witness and to serve more effectively

1. *The Church's Educational Ministry: A Curriculum Plan*, p. 807.
2. *Ibid.*
3. David Hunter, *Christian Education as Engagement*, p. 73.

7

Leadership in the Teaching Ministry

The tentative nature of the suggestions found in this book needs continual underscoring. In this connection it is important to be reminded again that the church is in the process of becoming. It might be comfortable, but actually quite dangerous, to assume arrival, that all answers are in, and that now we are able to crystallize the shape of the teaching ministry. Five years from now it may be abundantly clear that the directions suggested thus far, if followed, would have led to disaster. Nevertheless, it is enjoined upon us to think, to discuss, to pray, to work, and to attempt to discover what obedience in the teaching ministry requires in this time.

Crucial in this search are leaders. How are they called? How are they trained? What is required of them? Leaders with the view of a congregation as a people becoming, with an objective that focuses on ultimate purposes, and with a willingness to experiment with settings and variables, will be far different from the type of leader generally conceptualized, whose work can be neatly outlined in job descriptions and whose task is to keep a teaching agency going.

Few congregations are sitting on dead center. Those that are may be victimized by an entrenched power structure unable to cope with change. I remember a small congregation which seemed content to squabble. The ministry was in the hands of one family. The Sunday school was in the hands of the other family. The congregation moved through the decades in a stalemate. One day an older brother who had been Sunday school superintendent for twenty-five years was asked, "Do you think it's time that we look for another superintendent?" Immediately he replied, "Well, I don't see any timber coming along." With ministers in office "for life," obviously the Sunday school superintendent has to be in "for life" to keep things balanced. Then, too, twenty-five years of "superintending" that prepared no one to carry on reflects the kind of leadership provided.

Many leaders, both designated and undesignated, are needed in the teaching ministry. Teachers are an important part of the designated leadership group. We must learn a great deal more about those who are teaching presently, and we must try to discern the kind of teachers needed for the days ahead.

One denomination undertook a major research project to discover more about their teachers. Their findings are of great importance for future planning. They found, for example, that their typical teacher is a woman. She is between thirty and thirty-nine years of age. She had between one and three years of college. She has three children in the range of six to fourteen years of age. She has lived in the same home from sixteen to eighteen years. She is white (95 percent of the teachers are white). She has moved two times in her life, and in each case she moved from towns of less than a million people. Her husband is a professional person or a technician. She herself is a full-time housewife. Her annual income is in the $7,000 to $14,000 range. She gives between $3.00

and $3.99 to her church each week. This study helped the denomination see who is carrying on the teaching ministry and in turn what kind of help should be provided.

To learn that teaching is done by persons who are not mobile and who are white, upper-middle-class, may help to explain why churches are failing to broaden their membership, why they talk about evangelism, but do not move far from base.

The study noted above also found that the teacher teaches six to ten students; she has thirty-six to forty minutes for class period; she spends up to 1 1/2 hours in preparation; she had no pre-teaching training—she was just given a book and told to get to work; she does little evaluation of her teaching except when things go wrong; and she feels that to be sincere, to practice what you preach, and to love children are quite important for the teacher. Of less importance are church history, knowledge of doctrine, and concern about the mission of the church.

This study illustrates how seriously one denomination takes its teachers. Much time and expense were involved in learning about them. We do not have such information about Mennonite teachers. But it is needed if planning for the teaching ministry is to be supported with hard data rather than hunches.

Beginnings of Teacher Training

In the early days of the marriage between the public school and the Sunday school, teaching in both agencies had much to be desired. The teacher's qualifications were his knowledge of a subject and his ability to be a drill-master. For the public school teacher there developed the "normal school," as it was called, or the teacher-training school. This raised the level of teaching in the public school. But the Sunday school continued to use untrained volunteer teachers with only spasmodic attempts at teacher-training. Even Clarence Benson points out that Sunday schools suffered badly because of this. [1] It wasn't until 1862 that there is record of a teacher-training class. [2]

Among most Mennonites there were no teacher-training classes until near the turn of the century. A training class was held at Smithville, Ohio, in 1895 by a Brethren Church which Mennonites attended. This led to the sponsoring of a teacher-training class in the Oak Grove congregation, Smithville, Ohio, in 1897. The class met for a few evenings and disbanded. However, one of the persons who attended the 1895 training class wrote in the *Herald of Truth:*

During the past ten days the Dunkard brethren held a Normal Bible School [note the word "normal"—this was the word used for teacher-training] in the High School Academy building of Smithville, Ohio. A number of our brethren took advantage of the school. We must confess with a number of others that attended we only find how little we know about the one volume which is worthy of the name "the Book," whose central theme is "redemption." It gives Sabbath school teachers and Bible students new impetus. It makes Bible study more interesting. It gives the student a system of studying the "written Word." We feel the time is not far distant when all our churches will find the need of such Bible work which will open a new epoch in church history and create new fields of labor in the Master's harvest field, which is "white already to harvest." [3]

Feel the excitement. The correspondent awaits the day when all these things will happen. That was many years ago, and that dream is still to come true. Today the need for preparing leaders for the teaching ministry is as great as ever.

Kinds of Leaders

The word "leader" is ambiguous. Designated and undesignated leaders were mentioned above. The undesignated leader is the leader-member. This is any member of the group who by his actions helps members of the group move toward the attainment of their goals. In one set of circumstances one member emerges as leader; in another situation someone else serves. In each case the leader-member has the ability to move the group toward the goal.

The circumstances that call forth leader-members are varied, perhaps a crisis, an experiment or the need for information will call forth a leader. Each member has the responsibility to step into the leadership role when and where the group can utilize his particular contribution. It is also true that each member has the responsibility to subordinate his personal desires or needs when another member is better qualified to lead the group toward its goals. There is a sense in which every member at some time is a leader, carrying responsibility at a given time or place to help the group get on to a goal.

The designated leader is the formal leader or the appointed leader of a group. He is the person who has been asked through official procedures of the group or by the overall organization to perform a particular task. He may be asked to teach a Sunday school class, to serve as chairman of a committee, to administer a program. A designated leader is one who is called. He needs to study the responsibility he has been asked to assume, and to develop necessary skills to carry it out.

Perhaps another kind of leader, a kind we scarcely know how to deal with, should be mentioned—the prophet. In Chapter 1, prophets were seen as gifts of the Spirit, whose task was to proclaim the will of God in clear, comprehensible language. The congregation had better be ready to have some prophets around. The prophet, therefore, is a special kind of leader; he has an unmistakable call from God; his response is voluntary; he can't do anything except what he is doing. Prophets are rare; often little attention is paid to them. Sometimes it is difficult to recognize prophets. They are treated as were the prophets in ancient Israel, or as Christ was treated, or are written off as neurotic. The congregation must be open to the possibility that the Spirit of God is still raising up prophets. It would be well to let them speak and to hear what they say.

A designated leader is one who does not work *for* the group; rather, he is one who works *with* the group. This is important in a flexible program since the designated leader helps the group determine its goals and carry them out. The designated leader tries to become what the group needs him to be and he finds deep satisfaction in the joy of being used for God's purposes as they are revealed to his brethren. The designated leader is willing to take the risk of letting the group members grow. The old superintendent with twenty-five years' tenure might have been threatened had some young "timber" come along.

The designated leader must allow group members to question his assumptions, permit members to be critical of him and of the traditions. He does not let the worst kind of conduct in the group member give him a case of jitters, for he knows that rejection freezes the situation and causes members to resist help; so he goes on loving and accepting the group members even when they are unloving, irritating, or even revolting. Such a leader sits lightly in the saddle, not interfering, and at times employing planned neglect.

The designated leader wants to keep group members from becoming dependent upon him. He avoids the temptation to display how bright and resourceful he is by supplying needs and ready-made ideas. This is quite the opposite of Christian education leaders in days gone by. They were bright, resourceful persons, and had pamphlets and buttons and neat and tidy answers for anything the congregation wanted to do. This kind of leader is out because the congregation itself, as a people, is coming into being and the leader himself is a learner along with the rest. Sometimes he leans forward and gives guidance; sometimes he leans back and lets things happen. He yearns to help the group and to receive help. He learns from those in the group and attempts to release the resources in the group for the task at hand. This is a strange "job description" of a designated leader. In my files are pamphlets containing job descriptions for every office in the Sunday school. Every duty is outlined. The trouble is, they assume an agency with fixed variables. But they don't fit when a congregation is in transition to a more flexible teaching ministry focused on preparing persons for witness and service in the world, and developing program in the light of its situation, its gifts, and its readiness to be obedient.

Perhaps the place to begin training leader-members or designated leaders is with a depth study of the meaning of the gospel and the nature and mission of the church. This would be required of new as well as old members of the congregation. In this the pastor is strategic. He is knowledgeable theologically. This depth study would involve thorough exploration of the Old and New Testaments. In studying the Old Testament, today's leaders, like those in the early church, would see God, not as some abstraction, but as one who acts. In the New Testament they would see how Jesus lived. They would hear His sayings, and discover what He is calling men to. They would see that He calls, not to setting up ideals or to distilling principles, but to obedience. "If ye love me, keep my commandments."

Depth study would include church history. The congregation is a people coming into being. History helps leaders see how God has worked through His people across the centuries. It is not tracing the story of structures which people are asked to join.

Depth study would include the exploration of social issues from a Christian perspective. They would see how the cross brings reconciliation. They would study issues related to earning a living, to civic responsibilities, and to home relationships in the light of revelation.

Focus on Adults

Leadership education is really adult education. It is time to challenge the preoccupation of many congregations with children's education. Important as teaching children is, any teaching program focused primarily on children will be self-defeating. [4] Many congregations demonstrate this, especially "mission" congregations which have worked with children for years. There are many reasons for this. Child-oriented programs are handicapped by a serious shortage of trained leaders and teachers. Without an adult program there is no way to develop leadership among adults in the congregation. A children's program makes little contribution to a total community strategy. It makes the church one more handout agency, dealing on a surface level, and avoiding the basic issues. Further, emphasis on boys' clubs and girls' clubs and on other children's activities leaves little time for anything else. There is no end of children to serve and this keeps the church from dealing with the issues that trouble adults—and concerning which the gospel has something to say. Preoccupation with children suggests that the church is just for children—a babysitting establishment. As people say, "Sunday school is good for the kids."

Today, the church must focus on adults. There is a lot of sentimental talk about children who don't hear about the gospel, and about how much easier it is to win children. However, it is just possible that the kingdom will be extended more effectively if the church starts with adults who live as disciples in the world, who provide leadership, and who in turn make Christian homes. This, for some, is a long way around, since as they say, one can do almost anything with little children. Children are responsive and easy to work with, and in working with children, church workers avoid confrontation with adults. The worker's faith is not tested on the anvil of dialogue with adults. A little child seldom tests one's faith and presuppositions as does an adult. But this kind of testing is precisely what one's faith needs. Again, at the heart of leadership, preparation must be a broadly based, in depth, adult educational program.

Short-Term, Specific Tasks

A word about leadership recruitment. As suggested earlier, leaders should be recruited on the basis of their gifts and sense of call. They should be selected also in the light of the job to be done. Because of the experimental and flexible program envisioned, persons recruited must be able to absorb both praise and hostility. They must be healthy persons emotionally, physically, and spiritually. Since programs are flexible and experimental, leadership should be recruited on a short-term, for a specific project, basis. Currently, when a person is recruited to be a Sunday school teacher, his assignment may go on and on year after year. Perhaps teachers should be recruited for a specific course of study for a specific quarter or other designated period. This would assume special competence for a given study. Such recruitment may involve increased teamwork. As it is now, a person is asked to be a teacher, he is given a book and kissed good-bye until the next year, when either he is asked to do it again, or he resigns and someone else replaces him.

Recruitment requires seeing the teaching ministry as a whole. Each teacher needs support, information, counsel, and orientation. Planning must be done *with* teachers, not *for* them. This requires face-to-face activity. The pastor, since he is a theologically trained person, should orient teachers as individuals or as a group to the studies to be dealt with. Teachers in the junior and intermediate departments should have orientation to the annual themes— redemption, discipleship, and church. For a pastor to prepare teachers for teaching great biblical themes might be a better use of his training and his time than counseling. In counseling, he spends hour after hour with one troubled person. In teaching teachers, he frees resources of a large group for a more effective teaching ministry. Perhaps the congregation should provide therapeutic groups, thus allowing the minister to serve as a consultant, releasing the resources of the well for the tasks that are at hand.

Director of Christian Education

In the light of the foregoing discussion, it follows that the director of Christian education office should not be developed in our congregations. This office presupposes the coordination of teaching agencies. This office has served to confuse issues. It has not been successfully related to the work of the minister. Generally the educational director has been the low man on the totem pole. His work has been to set up departments and to administer projects. It would be better to have the pastor filling the teaching function and placing certain administrative responsibilities (which take a minister's time) with a congregational executive secretary. Obviously, the pastor cannot fill a larger teaching responsibility with a full administrative load. The best use of his theological training, however, is not to keep him busy in administration and then employ an educational director. An executive secretary would have a wide range of responsibilities. He would see to it that the building is repaired. He would do leg work for the curriculum and personnel committees. He would do scheduling and see to it that the weekly bulletin is published. He would gather announcements and coordinate visitation of the sick. This would free the minister to recover his teaching ministry, to be with the people, to teach, to listen, to hear. It would place his theological training at the disposal of the congregation. Thus, functioning when the church is gathered, the minister would be the trainer of laymen for ministry in the world when the church is scattered.

The congregation must provide for administration. But administration must be seen as administration. It should not be confused with education, nor should it confuse the role of the minister, especially when his role is an interpreter of Scriptures, a teacher of Christians on depth levels, an equipper of Christians for their mission in the world. The minister is a teacher of teachers, and a teacher of laymen. The layman is the minister of Christ in the world.

In summary, many leaders, member-leaders, and designated leaders are needed to assist the congregation toward its objective. Leaders emerge in response to needs, to gifts, and to call. The leadership needs of the congregation must be seen holistically. Leadership development requires a strong emphasis on teaching adults. The minister must fill a strategic role in training leadership.

Discussion Questions

1. To what extent do you agree with teachers who feel that to be sincere, to practice what you preach, and to love children are of greater importance than church history, knowledge of doctrine, and concern about the mission of the church?

2. Do you agree that the church must focus on teaching adults?

3. How can leadership in a congregation be evaluated and changed when necessary?

4. What is a "designated leader"? Have you noticed other kinds of leaders in your congregation?

5. Should a director of Christian education be appointed in your congregation?

1. Clarence Benson, *A Popular History of Christian Education*, p. 195.
2. Herbert Moninger, *Fifty Lessons in Training for Service* (1908), p. 63.
3. *Herald of Truth*, XXXII (March 15, 1895), p. 89.
4. See *Handbook on Christian Education in the Inner City*, by Lester W. McManis, for a helpful discussion of the importance of working with adults.

8

Curriculum for the Congregation

There are many definitions of curriculum. Here are several:

"A curriculum is a plan whereby the purpose of Christian education is to be achieved." [1]

"Curriculum," which originally meant a race course, is the path traversed by pupil and teacher in reaching a desired objective. . . . The basic curriculum is the whole of life, but the term is normally restricted to learning experiences under some kind of control by a responsible institution. . . . William Clayton Bower formulated a definition, which the International Council of Religious Education adopted in 1930: "the curriculum of Christian religious education is the experience of the learner under guidance."

Religious educators have accepted this interpretation, insisting that "method consists in bringing about those conditions under which enrichment and control of experience take place." The subject matter for such a curriculum develops from experience, utilizing the actual situation as well as the past experiences of the learners and teacher. Systematized and recorded knowledge from the past is brought to bear on the concerns of the present, so that the curriculum becomes a means for living meaningfully now and in the future. [2]

There are two valid ways of defining curriculum: the first of these may be termed the broader definition; the second the narrower.

[Speaking broadly] curriculum is . . . constituted by all of those media of communication and all those influences by which the less mature are nurtured within the Christian community and, it is hoped, brought into effective relation to God and made partakers of the body of Christ. . . . Curriculum is all of the media of communication and all of the influences by which the church brings itself to bear upon the individual in nurture.

[More narrowly] curriculum . . . refers to courses of study and, even more specifically, to study literature. Curriculum commonly refers, therefore, to the study materials deliberately designed and prepared as a central agent . . . in the Christian nurture of children, youths, and adults. [3]

Wyckoff defines curriculum as:

The plan and program by which the church seeks to fulfill its educational imperative. "Curriculum is experience under guidance toward the fulfillment of the purposes of Christian education—not the entire social situation within which the person acts and with which he is interacting, but rather that part of it which is consciously planned." The plan consists of educational procedures selected and used to help the learner to perceive, accept, and fulfill God's redeeming purpose in Jesus Christ. [4]

Following this definition, Wyckoff defines "program" as activities constituting the church's total educational ministry for children, youth, and adults, the family and the congregation as a whole. He points out that in most cases program is synonymous with curriculum as defined above and that the old administratively begotten distinctions between curriculum as materials and program as activities are specifically rejected.

Whether broad or narrow, we observe that: (1) Curriculum is a plan. (2) It has a purpose or objective. (3) It has subject matter which may be from experience or from recorded knowledge. (4) It consciously involves the media and influences of the church for nurture.

In a real sense, as the teaching ministry undergirds the mission of the church, so curriculum material undergirds the teaching ministry. To undergird, three things are necessary. (1) Curriculum must provide information, background, and understanding—in a word, orientation. (2) It must explain procedures. (3) It must provide for participation. [5]

There are at least five questions that are fundamental for understanding curriculum. They are: (1) Where is the curriculum? This is the question of *context*. (2) What is the curriculum? This is the question of *substance*. (3) What does the curriculum communicate? *Scope and comprehensiveness* is involved in this question. (4) How is the curriculum developed? This is the question of *process*. It involves an understanding of teaching, learning, and methods. (5) How is the curriculum organized? This is the question of relationship among various components. This is referred to as *organizing principle*.

The first question deals with *context*. Already we have seen the context as the congregation.

The nature of the congregation as gathered and scattered suggests something of the *substance* of curriculum.

When the church is gathered, orientation involves Bible study, doctrine, history, morality, and ethics. Procedures involve understanding how people relate in church administration, in binding and loosing, and in structuring and providing resources, printed or otherwise, for the teaching ministry. Participation is simply assuming responsibility in the teaching ministry, exercising one's gift, responding to the call. There is: (1) group prayer, (2) Bible study, (3) corporate worship, (4) listening to other Christians, and (5) an attempt to find ways to make the life of the congregation increasingly relevant to the life in the world. In worship and in nurture, Christians are brought to recognize the mission of the church, to reveal God's love for the world. Here Christians come to see that the church is called and sent to serve the world, not by the special tasks that Christians may engage in while the church is gathered, but mainly by the style of life—in word, deed, attitude—that affirms that Jesus Christ is Lord of all of life. Here the truth is impressed that the church has a ministry in the world and that it is carried out by each member when he is concerned about all men, when he is willing to accept all men as Christ did, when he is ready to share with men what God has done in Christ, when he invites men to Christ as Savior and Lord, and when he is concerned that there be justice and righteousness among men.

When the church is scattered, curriculum is required that will help members to carry out their ministry as witnesses and servants in the world, to confess Jesus as Lord, and to do deeds of love. Christ does not ask the Christian to withdraw from the world; rather, He sends him into the world. In order to witness in the world, the Christian needs orientation. For this, he will find useful his background of Bible study and doctrine, but service in the world requires orientation of another kind. This requires insight into the counsel of God concerning his occupation, concerning his responsibility as a citizen, concerning needs in the community and how they should be ministered to in the name of Christ. The Christian who is serving in the world deals with oppression, injustice, and violence. He is concerned that his home is different so that it can indeed be called a Christian home. He is concerned about the use of the material resources that he earns. He is concerned about a Christian standard of living and about his use of leisure time.

Participation in the world as a witness and servant, walking in the Spirit, fulfilling the call to discipleship— this is the *objective*. The objective of the church is the objective of Christian education and of curriculum. The moment the Christian moves from the gathered community in the meetinghouse to his neighborhood, to his home, and to his job, he has no alternative but to be Christian, to be a disciple of Jesus Christ. Increasingly, the congregation must realize that if one member fails, it is not only he who fails; it is the whole body. The curriculum must contribute to the realization that if one brother fails, all have failed in what he has done or failed to do.

The objective of Christian education points to the centrality of the Bible in curriculum: "to know God as revealed supremely in Jesus Christ and the Scriptures." To "know" means more than intellectual conceptualizations or abstractions. It means to be in relationship with or to experience another. God calls all men into such relationship with Himself. His redeeming acts are recorded and interpreted in Scripture. God sent His Son so that men would know what God is like and how He relates to men. At the same time He sent His Son to reveal what man should be like in all his relationships. Thus, "to know God," curriculum must confront persons with God's redemptive acts among men, with the person of Jesus Christ, and with salvation through faith in Him.

The Bible contains relational material, much of it in narrative form. These narratives are not abstract nor do they distort the truth. These narratives present men as they are—mixtures of good and evil. In spite of faithlessness and rebellion, God still comes to man, and calls him into relationship. Through the Bible, God reveals both Himself and the response He desires from man.

In the Anabaptist tradition, the Bible has always occupied a central place. It is seen as the inspired and authoritative Word of God, which through the Holy

Spirit is the infallible guide to lead men to faith in Christ and to guide in the life of discipleship. To be true to this tradition, curriculum must be deeply rooted in the Scriptures. On this, there is general agreement. How this is done, however, is not completely clear. On the one hand is the suggestion that we begin with persons where we perceive them to be, and in turn find passages of the Bible that are relevant to these needs and to this readiness. On the other hand, the person is seen in the midst of the congregation—the people of God coming into being that recognize the presence of God, that recite and celebrate God's great acts in history, and that see Him at work in the present age. Humbly and carefully the congregation shares with the individual the great events in the story of redemption, making him aware of the foundations of the fellowship of faith, and sharing with him the world view of the Bible in the light of the Bible's understanding of man, his need, and his worth. Both views recognize the importance of being aware of persons, how they grow and develop.

We are coming to see that curriculum materials also must begin with the believing community, gathered around the Word. The community relates and rehearses the acts of God which have provided the basis for the community. The curriculum attempts to root the person in the community's heritage, allowing God to speak as He will through relationships and the biblical record, while using the discoveries of the social sciences as tools for more effective communication. This posture, we hope, will keep our curriculum from violating either the person or the gospel.

This approach may help persons in the teaching ministry to be more relaxed, as they, in the context of the believing community, increasingly allow the Scriptures to speak for themselves and as they increasingly rely on the Holy Spirit to work in the lives of persons. The seeming tension between beginning with experience and beginning with content is reduced because of the realization (growing out of the experience of the church) that persons will find out about God, less as abstraction and more as person, as the Scriptures are opened in the light of their situation.

It is clear that many learnings are inherent in almost every passage of Scripture. Furthermore, there are many needs and varied experiences in every learner. To attempt to make a Bible story or a Bible passage speak to one specific need or problem, may stand in the way of the Bible's ability to speak to other issues, and may ignore the wide range of needs in the person beyond the one singled out. Attempts in previous curricula to make one-to-one relationships (one verse or passage to one need) are open to question, both from the standpoint of what Scriptures are able to say and from the standpoint of the wide variety of needs and experiences of persons. This is not to say that certain one-to-one relationships are not possible or even desirable, nor that they ought not be tried. It does suggest that confidence in the Word, in relationships, and in the Holy Spirit frees the teacher to expect learnings and experiences that could scarcely be anticipated, much less programmed. Thus, we are granted freedom to confront persons with the heritage of faith without confining the Scripture to specific "applications" nor confining the persons to the limitations of what certain observers have generalized about inner life and needs.

The objective begins with the Bible, but not as a textbook. Basically, it is not a book that is taught. Abraham did not have a book; the early church leaders did not have a book—they had events in which the reality of new relationships with God was evident. The task, therefore, is to communicate by word and deed the reality of the relationship with God and men as revealed in the Scriptures and in the heritage of the community of faith both in its history and in its present experience.

When it comes to process, curriculum must help the Christian tap the resources for witness and service that come from the Bible, from his brethren, and from the Holy Spirit. The Bible reveals what it means to be obedient. His brethren stand behind him in prayer; they give and receive counsel. He can turn to them for guidance. Thus, the Christian life is not a personal or individual matter. Indeed, the Christian may be alone geographically at work, or he may be the only Christian in his community, but still he is not alone, for he is undergirded by the prayers of the church and he belongs to a larger group so that at any moment of personal decision, he is part of the strategy of Jesus Christ and His church for the reconciliation of the world. Clearly, curriculum must provide for giving and receiving counsel, for sharing concerns, and for prayer one for another.

Space does not permit dealing with organizing curriculum. In conclusion, as curriculum is planned for congregations in the days ahead, several observations may be helpful:

1. Since the congregation is a group of people coming into being, and since each congregation has a different situation within which to minister and a wide range of gifts, the planning of the teaching ministry and the provision of undergirding curriculum will rely increasingly on local initiative. Christians in each congregation will need to think through what is needed in the teaching ministry in order to prepare Christians for their task. Furthermore, flexibility which this day demands will require that the

teaching program be less structured. Various groups will be studying areas of specific interest or need. An entire congregation studying a group of ten verses, as in the old Uniform Series plan, will likely diminish.

2. Earlier, it was noted that Christian education, in its primary sense, is teaching those who have come to know Christ all that He commanded. Education in its derived sense is providing necessary training and information for children of the congregation. As long as adults become members of the church and continue as members in the church, they will need education in the primary sense— learning what it means to be a follower of Jesus Christ. However, it may be necessary to establish a terminal for education in its derived sense. This terminal point for teaching children might be set for seventeen years of age. All that is planned for the Christian education of children would build toward that time in life when the individual leaves home, leaves the community, and strikes out on his own. Seventeen is the age when many young people go to college or to voluntary service, or shortly thereafter are caught up in the draft. In a real sense, whatever the congregation is able to do for the child in its teaching ministry has been done by seventeen. There is little more a congregation can do to present the claims of Christ or the Christian way of life. The congregation needs an overview of its teaching ministry from preschool through seventeen, so that at each step along the way and in each setting congregations can make available what the child needs to understand the gospel and what it means to be a follower of Jesus Christ in the world.

3. In the future, a great deal more evaluation must be done. Few congregations attempt to evaluate their teaching ministry. Three areas should be evaluated. First, structures should be evaluated. In a sense, this has been

the theme of these chapters. This involves analysis of the situation in which the teaching ministry takes place, and attempts to discover ways in which the variables can be recombined into new and more effective forms.

Second, process of the teaching ministry should be evaluated. Process includes an examination of what teachers do. It includes an examination of what pupils do. It includes an examination of how teachers and pupils interact in the various settings. For some people, process is most important in the teaching ministry. Certainly process is important if we take seriously the whole matter of relationships and especially the nature of relationships in the context of the community of faith.

Third, the product should be evaluated. Here there should be an attempt to measure kinds of change and degrees of change in the lives of pupils. The most simple kind of evaluation is measurement of Bible knowledge. This is not easily done, but many attempts have been made to create tests which measure a person's attainment in Bible knowledge. More difficult is the evaluation of spiritual growth. Even though difficult, most of us engage in this in informal ways. We note, for example, if someone seems "to grow" in his spiritual life. Most difficult is the evaluation of the development of Christian attitudes and values. Not a great deal of work has been done in this area. In addition the extent to which persons participate in the life and mission of the church as a result of the teaching ministry can be evaluated. In any case, evaluation must be an ongoing process. It should not be left to moments of crisis when the congregation wonders what went wrong.

Through these chapters we have covered a lot of territory—for the most part, too superficially and with too many generalizations. We have noted teaching among

God's people, the development of the present strategy, the crisis in Christian education, settings for Christian education, leadership in the teaching ministry, and finally, curriculum for the congregation. The purpose has been to focus on the teaching ministry in order to discern new directions for effectiveness and faithfulness today and in the days ahead.

Recently I attended a conference dealing with regional planning. One of the speakers who participated was involved in developing the regional plan for Washington, D.C. Because of the rapid population growth, expansion of government, increase in industry, planning had to be done to make the best use of that large area—2,300 square miles. The sprawl of Los Angeles was to be avoided, and they did not want the area to become one big waffle. A plan was evolved and it was a radical one. It involved open spaces, new cities in concentric circles with six arms of travel, radial corridors leading to new development areas.

The plan was presented over the name of the president of the United States, not as *the* plan, but as *a* plan for the area. Furthermore, the plan was billed for A.D. 2000. Thus, no one was threatened. Office seekers could fill their terms and even run for several more before 2000. As a result, people were able to look objectively at what ought to be. Once the plan was on the table, however, it had such force that it became the plan for the present. All municipalities in the area had to justify their refusal to follow the plan. Thus, without legislation, but only with the persuasive force of a good idea, the whole region is in the process of metamorphosis. To quote the speaker, "The plan withstood the apathy of the politician, the stupidity of the people, and the red tape of Washington."

We should take a page out of the planner's notebook. Today congregations must take a look at their teaching ministry as it is now and will be in the days ahead, perhaps in the year 2000, if the Lord tarries. The task is not to be critical of what was or now is; the task is to assess where the congregation is in its teaching ministry and what it needs to carry out its mission, and together, under the direction of the Holy Spirit, attempt to perceive where it should be going. These chapters have attempted, in broad outline, to suggest a direction the teaching ministry might take. We can be confident that, as Christians work together, plan together, think and pray together, the Lord of the church, through the Spirit He has sent, will lead the church to a faithful response to the Great Commission, "teaching them to observe all things whatsoever I have commanded you." The task is not to discuss reorganization as such. Rather, the task is to bring into focus what the teaching ministry of the church is, to gather needed data for present appraisal and future planning, and then in humility and in repentance for present failures to rely on God's grace not only for wisdom to plan aright but also for power to bring about change.

Discussion Questions

1. In the light of the various definitions of curriculum, how would you define "curriculum"?

2. Put in your own words the meaning of the following: "context," "substance," "scope and comprehensiveness," and "process" as these terms relate to curriculum.

3. How in the teaching ministry can we allow the Bible to exercise the authority it has instead of using the Bible as a source for good ideals and principles that we control for our purposes?

4. What issues are neglected in the teaching ministry of your

congregation? What does your congregation teach about oppression, injustice, and making moral and ethical decisions?

5. What changes do you anticipate in the teaching ministry in your congregation in the next decade, and how will you prepare for them?

1. *Presuppositions for the Development of a Curriculum for the Sunday Church Schools of the United Church of Canada*, p. 5.

2. Randolph Crump Miller, *Education for Christian Living*, pp. 43, 44.

3. J. Donald Butler, *Religious Education: The Foundations and Practice of Nurture*, pp. 262-64.

4. D. Campbell Wyckoff, *Theory and Design of Christian Education Curriculum*, p. 27.

5. For a full discussion of this see David R. Hunter, *Christian Education as Engagement*.

Selected Bibliography

Bender, Harold S. *These Are My People*. Scottdale, Pa.: Herald Press, 1962.

Boehlke, Robert R. *Theories of Learning in Christian Education*. Philadelphia: Westminster Press, 1962.

Butler, J. Donald. *Religious Education: The Foundations and Practice of Nurture*. New York: Harper and Row, 1962.

Cully, Kendig Brubaker. *The Search for a Christian Education —Since 1940*. Philadelphia: Westminster Press, 1965.

——————————(ed.). *The Westminster Dictionary of Christian Education*. Philadelphia: Westminster Press, 1963.

Fallow, Wesner. *Church Education for Tomorrow*. Philadelphia: Westminster Press, 1962.

Glen, J. Stanley. *The Recovery of the Teaching Ministry*. Philadelphia: Westminster Press, 1960.

Hunter, Archibald M. *Paul and His Predecessors*. Philadelphia: Westminster Press, 1961.

Hunter, David R. *Christian Education as Engagement*. New York: Seabury Press, 1963.

Kennedy, William Bean. *The Shaping of Protestant Education*. New York: Association Press, 1966.

Little, Lawrence C. *Foundations for a Philosophy of Christian Education*. Nashville: Abingdon Press, 1962.

Lynn, Robert W. *Protestant Strategies in Education*. New York: Association Press, 1964.

McManis, Lester W. *Handbook on Christian Education in the Inner City*. New York: Seabury Press, 1966.

Miller, Randolph Crump. *Education for Christian Living*. Englewood Cliffs, N.J.: Prentice Hall, 1956.

Muirhead, Ian A. *Education in the New Testament*. New York: Association Press, 1965.

Redekop, Calvin. *The Church Functions with Purpose*. Scottdale, Pa.: Herald Press, 1967.

Richards, Lawrence O. "Perspective on Purpose—Toward a Lean and Vital Structure for the Church," *United Evangelical Action*, Vol. 26, No. 6, July 1967.

————————. "Shape of Things to Come?—Toward a Lean and Vital Structure for the Church," *United Evangelical Action*, Vol. 26, No. 7, August 1967.

————————. "Strategy for Tomorrow—Toward a Lean and Vital Structure for the Church," *United Evangelical Action*, Vol. 26, No. 8, October 1967.

————————. "Twentieth Century Re-Formation—Toward a Lean and Vital Structure for the Church." *United Evangelical Action*, Vol. 26, No. 9, November 1967.

Roth, Arnold. *Learning to Work Together*. Scottdale, Pa.: Herald Press, 1967.

Selwyn, Edward Gordon. *The First Epistle of St. Peter*. London: Macmillan, 1952.

Sherrill, Lewis Joseph. *The Rise of Christian Education*. New York: Macmillan, 1944.

Smart, James D. *The Teaching Ministry of the Church*. Philadelphia: Westminster Press, 1954.

Studer, Gerald C. *Christopher Dock: Colonial Schoolmaster*. Scottdale, Pa.: Herald Press, 1967.

The Church's Educational Ministry: A Curriculum Plan, the work of the Cooperative Curriculum Project. St. Louis: Bethany Press, 1965.

Wenger, J. C. *The Church Nurtures Faith*. Scottdale, Pa.: Herald Press, 1963.

Wyckoff, D. Campbell. *Theory and Design of Christian Education Curriculum*. Philadelphia: Westminster Press, 1961.

The Author

Paul M. Lederach was born at Norristown, Pa. He was ordained as minister in the Mennonite Church in 1944 and as bishop in 1949. He has served pastorates in eastern Pennsylvania.

He took his undergraduate work at Goshen College and in 1946 received his ThB from Goshen College Biblical Seminary. He received his MRE degree in 1947 from Eastern Baptist Theological Seminary, Philadelphia, Pa., and his DRE in 1949 from the Southwestern Baptist Theological Seminary, Fort Worth, Texas. In 1965-66 he spent a year at the University of Pittsburgh under a Religious Education Association—Lilly Endowment Postdoctoral Empirical Research Training Fellowship.

For seven years he was field secretary of the Mennonite Commission for Christian Education and in 1965 was elected president of the Mennonite Board of Education.

He has served as editor of the Herald Uniform Sunday School Series, *Herald Teacher,* and *Family Worship,* and with Willard Claassen, co-edited the Mennonite Graded Sunday School Series.

He has written curriculum materials and articles in the field of Christian education, and has served as consultant for various publications and Christian education activities in the Mennonite Church. He is the author of *Learning to Teach,* one of the publications in the Christian Service Training Series of the Mennonite Church and General Conference Mennonite Church. Since 1961 he has been Director of Curriculum Development at the Mennonite Publishing House, Scottdale, Pa.